A VIOLENT END

Dansk started as a drip of water splashed down on the side of his head. Lifting the match higher, he could see where the water was soaking through from the bluff above, pooling on the cavern ceiling before falling in a slow but steady drip.

Strange. The water has a greenish hue, with streaks of darker color—almost emerald—twisting and rolling inside it.

Then the dying match picked out the exit hole's dark edges, and Dansk froze, unable to believe what he was seeing. His mouth opened in a soundless scream. The match died and plunged him back into darkness.

His thoughts churned, trying to make sense of this. Hands trembling, he lit another match.

The bloody, severed head still lay against the wall.

OTHER BOOKS IN THE SERIES

SMALLVILLE: STRANGE VISITORS

SMALLVILLE

DRAGON

ALAN GRANT

Superman created by
Jerry Siegel and Joe Shuster

WARNER BOOKS

An AOL Time Warner Company

WARNER BOOKS EDITION

Copyright © 2002 by DC Comics
All rights reserved under international copyright conventions. No part of this book may be reproduced in any form or by any electronic or mechanical means, including information storage and retrieval systems, without permission in writing from DC Comics, except by a reviewer who may quote brief passages in a review. Inquiries should be addressed to DC Comics, 1700 Broadway, New York, New York 10019.

Cover design by Don Puckey
Book design by L&G McRee

Warner Books, Inc.
1271 Avenue of the Americas
New York, NY 10020

Visit our Web site at
www.twbookmark.com.

Visit DC Comics on-line at keyword DCComics on America Online or at http://www.dccomics.com.

 An AOL Time Warner Company

Printed in the United States of America

First Printing: November 2002

10 9 8 7 6 5 4 3 2 1

For Robert Dylan Wofford
1976–2002

SMALLVILLE

DRAGON

PROLOGUE

The swarm of meteorites rolled and tumbled through the vast, velvet darkness of space. A hundred or more chunks of rock spinning in their own personal orbits, every orbit in synch with every other as they streaked through the cosmos at ten miles per second.

They'd entered the solar system months earlier, arcing in past Pluto and the frozen outer worlds on their long journey toward destruction and death. They swept in past Jupiter, deflected like a slingshot by the effects of the giant's crushing gravity. Sunlight glinted from the tumbling rocks as they plunged toward the inner planets like a dark, spinning necklace of doom.

Toward the blue planet. Earth.

At the heart of the swarm—as if it was the meteors' purpose to protect it—was a tiny metallic spacecraft.

Disguised by its grim guardians, no satellite would track the craft. No radio telescope would detect its presence. No astronomer would ever see it.

They spiraled past the Moon, disdainful of its lack of atmosphere and lifeless surface. Then Earth's gravity seized control, and the meteors blazed fiery red as they flashed down through the stratosphere toward the world that shimmered far below.

In the heart of Kansas corn country, like a sparkling jewel itself under impossibly blue prairie skies, the town of Smallville was celebrating Homecoming Day. WELCOME TO THE

CREAMED CORN CAPITAL OF KANSAS, read the sign that
straddled the town limits.

Out on the perimeter, where the roads disappeared
straight as arrows between the fields of swaying corn, billionaire Lionel Luthor had taken his nine-year-old son, Lex,
to witness his latest business deal. He'd just bought the old
corn factory from the Ross brothers, with a verbal guarantee
he'd keep the factory open. What would be the point of
telling them the truth? Smallville's corn capital status had
been on the wane for years, as giant farms owned by pen-
sions funds, banks, and insurance companies—whose stock-
holders might never have tasted creamed corn in their
lives—took over the land in other parts of the country.

The small farms were struggling for survival. Lionel
Luthor knew there was no way they could compete. They
had to diversify, find new ways to earn a living from the rich
Kansas soil. So did he. That's why his new fertilizer plant,
one of the most advanced in the world, would be built here.

So what if it meant breaking a promise? Men could
promise each other anything they wanted, but at the end of
the day it was the lawyers who would decide. Economics
ruled the world. If people couldn't afford to buy food, and
clothes, and seed corn for next year . . . what did it matter
what they produced and sold? Ordinary men did what economics forced them to.

Lionel Luthor had long since learned how to apply the
rules to his own life and business. He hadn't become a billionaire because he kept his promises.

But the omens in the skies were not good.

Trailing sparks and flaming dust and smoke, the mass of
meteors screamed through the atmosphere, its temperature
rapidly increasing.

Jonathan and Martha Kent giggled like teenagers as they
headed out of town in their pickup truck. They'd loaded the

four-by-four with a week's supplies, and waved to the celebrating townsfolk as they headed out on the narrow back road that would take them home.

Farming wasn't an easy life, but it was the life they wanted, the future they'd chosen from all the opportunities open to them. Only one thing was lacking, only one prayer remained to be answered.

They both desperately wanted a child. But, seemingly, that desire was denied to them.

"Jonathan—look!"

Martha leaned forward, craning her neck to get a better view through the windshield. High above, lines of fire and trailing smoke had appeared in the sky.

Jonathan followed her gaze. His first thought was that it was an airplane in difficulty. But surely a plane wouldn't have disintegrated into so many pieces? And surely they couldn't all have caught fire?

A blazing meteor the size of a football streaked a hundred feet above their heads, surprising Jonathan so he almost lost control of the vehicle. The object was heading back the way they'd just come. To town.

Then the air was full of them, an impossible tapestry of burning, smoking threads. Through the open cab windows the Kents could smell scorched air and sulfurous fumes.

Suddenly, something flashed straight across the road in front of them, spitting flame and foul black smoke. There was a noise like a bomb exploding as it smashed down into a cornfield.

Blast waves shot out to engulf the car.

Jonathan braked and spun the steering wheel, but it was too little, too late. The pickup lurched violently across the road, sliding onto its side as it left the road and hit the field. It shuddered and shook as the four-wheel drive struggled to find purchase on the loose soil, then rolled over onto its roof.

Dazed and bewildered, wondering if this was the end of the world or merely the outbreak of war, Jonathan and Martha hung upside down in their seats, held securely by their safety belts. Martha stared out of the cracked windshield, unable to believe her eyes.

A child, naked and unafraid, stared back in at her.

Frantically, the Kents fought their way free. As Martha stooped to comfort the child, Jonathan raced into the field of flattened corn. There might be others there, survivors of whatever disaster had just befallen.

What he found there would change their lives forever.

Destruction rained like biblical Armageddon on the small town.

A water tower exploded, its contents instantly vaporized as a meteor smashed into it. Part of the bank's upper stories crumbled into rubble. A young couple getting out of their car on Main Street disappeared in a searing fireball.

The meteors altered everything, forever, bringing changes nobody would understand for a long, long time. Bringing destruction and death.

And, in the strangest way possible, bringing hope for all mankind.

CHAPTER 1

TWELVE YEARS LATER

Monday Morning

Metropolis Penitentiary stood like some grim, gray futuristic fortress, its vast bulk rising five stories over the surrounding flatlands.

High atop the walls, powerful searchlights swept back and forth in a never-ending circuit, turning the deepest shadows to brightest day wherever their beams struck. In the concrete towers that protruded from the corners of the razor-wire-topped walls, bleary-eyed guards did their best to stay awake. Another half hour and night shift would be over. Until tomorrow night.

Inside the prison's Long Term Block, the tiers of steel-doored cells were silent. In the corridors, the lights that burned twenty-four hours a day shone with steady light. It had been several years since there was a successful escape, but the prison had to act as if there might be one every night, of every week, of every year.

The first of the day shift guards were supervising as the kitchen crew—made up of prisoners—threw off sleep and began preparing breakfast. On the lowest floor, the tier guards were preparing to be relieved by their daytime colleagues.

In his cell, Prisoner 2923/89, Raymond Dansk, was already awake. He splashed his face with cold water, feeling the droplets trickle down his neck and onto the fierce dragon tattoo that covered half his chest. He toweled himself dry and pulled on his gray prison drabs, leaving shirt and jacket open to the waist.

Sheets and blankets already stowed in his locker, he sat on the bare, metal-framed bed that took up the whole of one cell wall, and waited.

If there's one thing this stinking place has taught me, it's how to wait.

With practiced ease, his fingers teased a thin line of strong tobacco from a plastic pouch. Sprinkling it onto a cigarette paper, he rolled it with a smooth twist of his thumbs and raised it to his mouth. He had to moisten his lips before running his tongue along the gummed paper. He sparked a match, cupping it with his hands as he raised it to the cigarette.

He sucked tobacco smoke deep into his lungs and coughed once. His mind wouldn't engage until that first hit of nicotine was coursing through his bloodstream. Smoking was a habit he'd meant to break while he was cooped up. But prison was a lonely place, and often a cigarette was the only friend he had. He smoked more now than he had when he was first admitted.

Twelve years ago, Dansk thought. *A long time in anybody's terms.*

Twelve years missing from his life. Twelve years of ducking and diving, avoiding the yard-gangs, abusive guards, and the hard men who made it their business to violently stamp their authority on their fellow inmates.

Twelve years of paranoia and fear and keeping his head down.

Long enough to regret the crime that had sent him here, though the nightmares about the man whose life he'd taken had long since ceased. Long enough for Ray Dansk to decide that, whatever happened, he would never, ever do anything that might mean he'd be sent back to prison again.

Outside, the tiers were coming alive with the sounds of coughing and cursing. It must be dawn—though sunlight was never seen in the windowless cells. From far away, coming closer, he heard the distant clash of metal as the breakfast trolleys began to move to their destinations.

Dansk was just finishing his cigarette, stubbing it out in the tiny sink, when the cell light blazed on. A key rattled in the door lock, and the door swung open soundlessly.

A pudgy face sneered at him. "Not like you to be up before you have to be," a cold voice grated. "Must be a big day, right, Dansk?"

"Yes, Officer Wills, sir," Dansk said automatically. He'd long since perfected the old prison trick of keeping his eyes and voice neutral, a necessity in an environment where hatred, frustration, and fear could boil over almost instantly into physical confrontation. Funny how some of the guards always tried to needle the cons. Rise to the bait, and you could be on a charge that would add another month or two to your sentence, and get you thrown in the Hole for good measure. "It's my release date."

"If you're lucky, Dansk." Wills's eyes darted around the cell, and Dansk knew he was looking for something that would justify his foul temper. "It's a long way from here to the gate. Put one foot wrong, and you'll be staying on awhile."

Finding nothing to complain about, Wills glared at Dansk's chest, exposed by his open shirt. "Cover yourself up," he snapped. "There ought to be a law against prisoners mutilating themselves."

Dansk bit back the urge to ball his fist and smash it into the young officer's flabby face. It was the type of emotional reaction that had sent him here in the first place. He wouldn't make the same mistake twice. "It's a tattoo, sir," he said lamely, masking the contempt he felt. "I had it when I came in." He didn't know what Wills's problem was, but every con on the block knew that the officer was a bully who took perverse pleasure in making their lives as difficult as possible. The tattoo had seemed such a good idea at the time. He and the boys, the town's first biker gang. The Dragons, they called themselves. Now, the ink was old and fading; but still, it reminded him of the life he used to have.

He was buttoning his shirt when the wheels of the breakfast trolley squealed to a halt outside his cell.

Wills stood back reluctantly, to allow Dansk to step forward and take a chipped plastic tray from the trolley. Plastic bowl of cereal. Carton of milk. Three slices of toasted bread that had already gone cold, and a scoop of something the guards called margarine but the cons knew as grease.

Plastic spoon, plastic spreader, plastic mug. Nothing with a sharp edge. The sharpest things in jail, so the old joke went, were the prisoners' wits.

"Going home, eh?" Wills sneered, as Dansk sat down on the bed with the tray on his knee. "Ten bucks says you'll be back here inside a month. Your type never changes."

Don't let him rile you. "I committed the crime, I did the time. My debt is settled."

"You got ten minutes to eat," Wills said, finally tiring of trying to goad him. "Be ready when I come back for you— or it won't be today we stick you on a train back to . . . where is it again? Hicksville, Idaho?"

"Smallville, sir," Ray Dansk told him. "Smallville, Kansas."

Jonathan Kent leaned against the old barn and watched his son at work.

The fifteen-year-old was chopping logs, working so fast that the eye could barely follow him. He picked up a section of tree trunk and placed it on the ancient stump that served as chopping block, bringing the heavy Swedish ax down on it precisely. He stooped to grab the split logs and tossed them on the stack under the lean-to against the barn wall.

And all before Jonathan could count up to three.

Jonathan shook his head in wordless admiration and ran his fingers through his sandy hair. He watched for a moment more, marveling at the boy's amazing abilities, before calling out to him.

"Breakfast's ready, Clark."

Clark tossed an unsplit log into the air. Wielding the ax in one hand as if it was light as a walking cane, he quartered the log with two superfast strokes. He dropped the ax, caught the four sections before they hit the ground, and sent them spinning like Frisbees onto the stack.

"Still about a ton to do, Dad." Clark gestured to the trailerload of logs that had been upended in the farmyard. "A couple of minutes should be enough."

Just watching him made Jonathan visibly swell with pride. *Clark's my son,* he thought, *my incredible boy who can do things no man can even dream of doing.*

Smiling slightly to himself, Jonathan turned and ambled back to the screen door leading into the warm, old-fashioned farmhouse kitchen.

His wife Martha was whipping up waffle mix, using flour milled from their own small patch of wheat and milk from their own cattle. Even the blueberry jelly was made from fruits she'd grown, harvested, and cooked herself on the kitchen's log-burning stove.

Jonathan walked up behind her and let his arms encircle her waist. He leaned forward to kiss her gently behind the ear, then stood back, twitching his nose. Her hair did that every time.

Martha turned her head to smile at him, then wriggled

free of his grip. "Hey, I'm a working woman," she teased. "No time for canoodling."

"Canoodling." Jonathan repeated the word, let it roll around his tongue. "Long time since I heard anybody say that."

"Too old-fashioned," Martha replied, dropping a blob of batter onto the waffle iron. Perfect temperature. "Life's too fast for folks to canoodle anymore. They neck, or even"—she shuddered—"lock lips."

"Don't have quite the same ring to them, do they?" Jonathan whipped the coffeepot off the stove just as it started to boil, filling the room with its rich aroma. "Me, I think I'll settle for old-fashioned," he said, pouring the hot liquid into three mugs Martha had already set out on the table.

Martha took the first waffles from the iron, heaping them on a plate on top of the stove to keep them warm. "Clark?" she queried.

Jonathan added a dribble of milk to his coffee before replying. "Is chopping enough logs to last us at least a year. He should be here right about . . . now."

He'd barely got the word out when Clark appeared in the kitchen doorway.

"Great way to work up an appetite," the boy said. He went to the sink to wash his hands and sniffed the air appreciatively. "Mom, did anybody ever tell you you're the best cook in the world?"

"Your father did, once." Martha smiled as she carried the plate of waffles to the table and set them down. "Why do you think I married him?"

Jonathan sighed. "Here was me thinking it was because of my good looks and irresistible charm. Oh"—he gestured to the window, through which they could see past the wood-slatted bulk of the barn to the fields of swaying corn beyond—"and the undoubted charms of the rambling Kent acreage, of course."

The telephone rang, and Martha excused herself to lift the wall-mounted receiver.

"I'll tell him, Nell," Jonathan heard her say. "Good-bye."

Martha returned to the table and pushed another waffle onto Clark's plate. "That was Nell Potter. Lana's horse has escaped from the meadow again. If he comes around our way, can we tether him till she can send someone over."

Jonathan nodded. "I'll be out in the east fields this morning. I'll keep my eyes open."

"No need, Dad." Clark swallowed the last of his breakfast and got to his feet. "I'll find him. Right now."

"You don't have time," Martha protested. "You'll miss the school bus. Again."

"Start the stop clock."

Jonathan shook his head ruefully. Where Lana was concerned, Clark would happily miss the bus every morning.

Clark went out through the porch door and into the farmyard. They didn't often get visitors out here, so far off the beaten track, but he glanced cautiously around him anyway. He knew that he was different from everybody else, and of course his parents knew. But they had always taught him that his secret must stay exactly that. *Secret*.

Chickens scratched about in the farmyard soil, and a dozen ragged crows perched in the top branches of the old chestnut tree his father had never had the heart to uproot. "It was part of this landscape long before I came along," Jonathan had told him, "and it'll still be part of it when I'm long gone. It has as much right to be here as we have."

Apart from the cattle grazing in the adjacent meadow, there was no other sign of life.

As he reached the dirt track leading to the highway a couple of miles away, Clark began to run.

Instantaneously—and almost effortlessly—he was traveling at sixty miles per hour. The rest of the world seemed to slow down as he sped by. He could see every individual ear of corn as it waved slightly in the morning breeze. He saw a rabbit prick up its ears and turn toward him. But he was past it before the creature even realized there was any reason to be startled.

Calculating his trajectory with perfect precision, Clark leaped lithely into the air. He landed on a roadside fence post, immediately jumping onto the next before his weight caused the first to overbalance.

He gauged his pace to match the fence posts' unvarying regularity, then looked around. Even from this slight vantage height, he could see for miles over the flat cornfields. No sign of Lana's big chestnut roan.

The Potter place was only a mile away, a large country house set in acres of green lawns. There were a riding stable and pasture adjoining, and this wasn't the first time Lana's horse had found his way out.

Clark jumped back down onto the track and came to a standstill. There were half a dozen places the horse might have headed for. The grove of beech trees by the old well. The stand of willows growing out of the stream bank. But they lay farther out. The animal wouldn't have had time to get there.

Concentrating hard, Clark closed his eyes and listened intently. Like his strength and his speed and his vision, Clark's hearing was far beyond the range of ordinary mortals.

There, about half a mile distant. A faint whinny. At Bow Creek, a chunk of marshy ground that had recently been sold to a developer. In town they were already talking about the new housing development that was scheduled, if the zoning board gave the nod.

Clark covered the half mile in less than thirty seconds.

There was a natural depression in the ground here, where the creek ran into the Smallville River. It flooded during high water, and for the rest of the year, except midsummer, it was a marsh the locals knew to avoid. Willows and twisted birches grew around its fringes, and when Clark and his buddies were kids exploring the world, they'd whispered to each other that the deep pools of black, brackish water had no bottom. Fall in there, and you'd be sucked right down to the center of the Earth.

The horse whinnied again, sounding terror-stricken.

Clark moved forward carefully, treading from one clump of reeds to the next. He found it behind a tableau of dead trees and stunted bushes, its hind legs up to the haunches in thick, clinging marsh. Its front legs scraped desperately at drier ground as it tried to get a foothold to haul itself out. Its eyes rolled in its head, and its neck dripped perspiration.

"Easy, boy. I'll soon have you out."

But easier said than done. He couldn't pull the frightened beast by its front legs, for fear of injuring it.

He stepped up to the nearest tree trunk, a piece of deadwood twenty feet high, its side branches long since rotted and fallen. He pushed his back against it, muscles straining under his white T-shirt.

There was a loud crack as the trunk snapped and fell with a wet thud. Clark gripped one end and dragged it toward the stricken horse as if it were almost weightless. Maneuvering the heavy log with easy precision, he shoved it under the animal's front legs.

With something to offer resistance, the roan scrambled a few feet before falling back. It whinnied pitifully, then tried again. This time Clark was ready to help. One arm locked around the base of the horse's neck, and he exerted his strength to give the extra impetus it needed.

The horse climbed onto dry ground, stamping its hooves and tossing its head.

"Lana," Nell Potter called to her niece from the porch. "Visitor for you."

In the kitchen, Lana Lang was gathering the books she'd need for school that day. Who would be calling on her at this time of morning? She dumped her satchel on a chair and hurried out to the porch.

Her aunt Nell was sitting in a cane chair, drinking her morning fruit juice, laughing to herself at the figure approaching over the manicured lawns. "Looks like you found a white knight," she joked. "Only he's not so white."

Lana ran down the steps to the lawn, surprised to see her neighbor and classmate Clark Kent leading Czar toward the house. Clark's jeans and white T-shirt were stained with mud, and his thick black hair was soaking wet, nearly plastered to his scalp.

"I found him down at Bow Creek," Clark said by way of greeting. "He . . . uh, he almost got trapped in the marsh."

Lana wagged an admonishing finger at Czar and shook her head. The horse was obedient and docile most of the time, but when Czar took it into his head not to cooperate, there was nothing anyone could do. Which is what had happened this morning when he bolted from the meadow after her morning ride.

Lana looked Clark up and down. "He obviously had fun with you before you caught him, judging by the state you're in."

Clark flushed, and Lana went on hastily: "Sorry, I should at least thank you before I insult you. It's just—well, you *are* in a state. And the school bus will be calling at your place—"

she glanced at her wristwatch—"in approximately one minute."

"I seem to make a habit of missing it." Clark sighed. "Suppose I better go . . ."

He turned on his heel, but Lana rested her hand lightly on his arm. "I mean it—I really am grateful, Clark." She tilted her head up, and her lips brushed his cheek. "See you at school," she told him, as he started to leave. "That is, if you make it today!"

Clark felt light-headed as he made his way across the lawn. Lana had kissed him!

Okay, it was only on the cheek. But she was the prettiest girl in school, and Clark had been in love with her for as long as he could remember. Only trouble was, his feelings weren't reciprocated. She liked him as a friend—she'd told him often enough—but romance was strictly for her and her boyfriend, Whitney Fordman. Star athlete. Quarterback of the football team. Two years older than Clark, two years more mature.

He vaulted over the fence into the head-high cornstalks, where he couldn't be seen, and with his heart singing, ran as fast as he could along the rows.

It took him all of two minutes to race home, explain to his parents, have his second shower of the morning, change into clean clothes . . . and miss the school bus.

He could have asked Mom or Dad to give him a ride, but they had better things to do with their time. It was tough work, running the farm, doing their best to ensure it turned a profit. He hated to bother them with such a silly thing.

Besides, when you could run as fast as he could, there were other ways of getting to school.

It was twenty minutes before the school bus pulled up in front of the modern building that was Smallville High. The driver opened the doors and a gaggle of chattering teenagers came storming out.

Pete Ross was the first to step down. He did a double take as he saw his friend Clark seated on the school steps, studiously reading over their assignment from last week's philosophy class.

"Whoa," he said, eyes opening wide. "If it isn't the late Clark Kent. Lana told us you'd be lucky to make it before lunchtime."

Clark smiled enigmatically, and Pete turned to Chloe Sullivan. "You owe me five bucks," he said, holding out a hand. "I had every faith that my friend Clark, having rescued an equine in distress, and despite appearing to have missed the bus, would actually and very cleverly have arranged alternative transport. Am I right, my man?"

Clark grinned in return. "Something like that," he agreed. "So what's the hot gossip from the morning rocket ride?"

Pete watched Chloe toss her blond hair back from her face as she sat down on the stone steps beside Clark. He loved it when she did that. Made her seem so cool and sophisticated.

"An in-depth discussion of last week's football game, followed by in-depth anticipation of Lex Luthor's party this coming weekend," Chloe said scornfully. "Not a word about what we should have been discussing—contents of the next issue of the *Torch*."

"You city girls," Pete said. "Just can't adjust to country life, can you?"

Chloe had moved to Smallville in middle school, leaving her previous life in the big city behind. And not many cities were bigger than Metropolis. Pete remembered how she'd had difficulty adjusting to small-town life at first. Now, she'd settled in to Smallville, population 45,001. She channeled her considerable energy into the school newspaper she edited and put out every month.

"There just isn't a lot happening school-wise that compares with a major football game," Pete protested. "Plus, how many teenagers in this wonderful country get invites to a party in a genuine Scottish castle?"

"That might be cool if the castle was in Scotland," Chloe rejoined. "But, like, on the outskirts of town . . . ? Spare me."

A half dozen pickup trucks roared into the yard, the older pupils driving themselves to school. Clark and Chloe got to their feet and slowly began to climb the stairs toward the entrance.

As they reached the top of the stairs, Clark turned. His eyes strayed back toward the bus and lit up as he saw Lana coming through the door. She'd brushed her dark auburn brown hair until it shone, and her smile was the sweetest Clark had ever seen.

Beside him, Chloe shook her head. "Time for Clark's morning sigh," she said to Pete, but loudly enough for Clark to hear. "Can't take his eyes off her."

"And she's booked up for all eternity," Pete replied. He raised his voice. "Come on, Clark, we'll be late."

Clark nodded, though his gaze was firmly fixed on Lana. There was just something about her that made him—and half the other guys in school—go weak at the knees.

Lana looked up and saw him, and gave a smile and a little wave. Clark's heart beat faster in his chest. Maybe he should hang back, strike up a proper conversation with her. He hadn't exactly been scintillating when he returned Czar.

She was walking toward him, and he tried to prepare himself. Trouble was, his brain went all to pieces when he was around her.

At the last moment he noticed the sparkling, dark green

necklace Lana sometimes wore. He knew the story well: Lewis and Laura Lang had been the only fatalities that day twelve years ago, when the meteors hit Smallville like an enemy missile attack. The Langs had just got out of their car on Main Street, on their way to pick up three-year-old Lana from Laura's sister, Nell Potter.

In full view of Nell and Lana, the car had exploded in a gout of flame and smoke as one of the meteors struck. Lana's parents never stood a chance.

A small green stone—a fragment of the fatal meteor—had been the only memento of that terrible afternoon. When she'd grown older, Lana had it made into a necklace. She'd once told Clark it comforted her to have this reminder of the parents she could scarcely remember, but would never forget.

"So much bad luck came out of it," she'd said. "There can only be good luck left."

But from Clark's point of view, the necklace had a far deadlier "luck." He had gradually learned that, whatever mineral the meteors were made from, it had an effect on him unlike anything else. Somehow, the strange green matter weakened his powers and made him ill, reducing him to a confused, perspiring wreck.

The green stone had the power to hurt—even kill—him.

"Hi, hero." Lana stopped a couple of feet away. Her voice was warm and friendly. "Got your ride after all, then?"

Ironic, Clark thought. *The one thing in the world I want is to get close to Lana . . . yet if I do, that necklace will cripple me!*

He was wracking his brains for some witty reply when a well-built figure sprinted up the steps and came to a halt beside Lana. She turned toward him, and he bent to kiss her lightly on the lips.

Clark's heart sank. Whitney Fordman. Golden boy, all-conference quarterback, drives his own late-model pickup. How could he ever compete with Whitney?

Maybe if I could show her what I'm really capable of . . . But the thought died stillborn. His parents had always taught him that his amazing abilities—and even more amazing origin—must remain a total secret from everyone except the three of them. Clark might be able to beat the whole football team single-handed, but nobody—not Lana, or Pete, or Chloe—would ever know that.

Hand in hand, Lana and Whitney made their way into the school.

Clark followed, frustrated and resigned.

After twelve years in jail, the world seemed like a different planet.

The sky was unnaturally blue, the fields so green it was like seeing them for the first time. Everything had taken on a three-dimensional aspect again, after the 2-D existence that passed for life in the pen.

Ray Dansk leaned back in his seat in the train's dining car and gazed out the window at freedom. Blue skies and sunshine, not a cell bar or armed guard in sight. His liberty money had bought him a great meal—but everything seemed so much more expensive now than when he'd been put away. It wasn't going to last. First thing he'd do was find a job.

He was surprised by the number of new housing developments springing up in the countryside they passed through. STARTER HOMES FROM $250,000! blared from one billboard they sped past. A quarter million . . . for a house near Smallville?

Yeah, obviously changed days.

He glanced around the car at his fellow passengers. A half dozen men in business suits, scattered throughout the car, were talking into cell phones. "Hi, honey, I'm just passing a field of corn," he imagined them saying. A young man in navy uniform was sucking on a bottle of beer, his fifth or sixth since the journey began.

And then there was the girl.

Tall, blond, and voluptuous, she stood against the bar sipping iced tonic water. Her black jacket and orange skirt fit her perfectly. She wore black shoes with inch-high heels which she didn't really need, because her legs were long and shapely.

Twelve years since he'd even seen a woman, if he discounted the crone who taught the GED classes he'd attended. He only went to the first couple, anyhow.

A woman like this screamed "quality." She was obviously used to a life that went far beyond anything Ray Dansk ever hoped for.

He considered joining her at the bar. No, a woman like that wouldn't look twice at a man like him. He'd never been a great success with the opposite sex. The girls he liked never seemed to like him; and the few who did like him were dogs.

What the heck, she's traveling alone. Might be interested in some diversionary company. Besides, she hadn't spoken to anyone else, just leaned on the counter and stared out the window as if she'd never seen fields or cattle before. And hey, didn't Ray Dansk have some good stories to tell?

Plucking up his courage, he slid out of his seat and walked the few paces to the bar. He fought to keep his voice even, though his stomach was churning with butterflies. Twelve years is a long time.

"Can I buy you a drink?" he asked pleasantly.

She looked him over as if he was something she'd recently trodden in. "No." Her answer was curt and her voice frosty.

She didn't even turn her back on him, just went back to staring out the window.

Ray Dansk felt like the biggest jerk in Kansas.

The morning was taken up with math and physics, classes at which Clark excelled. His understanding of these subjects was years in advance of his classmates. His mental abilities—at least in certain areas—seemed to be on a par with his physical attributes.

But like his physical prowess, he had always had to be careful not to seem too far ahead of the others. In case it made them, or his teachers, suspicious.

Sitting in Mrs. Bartsen's math class, listening to stuff he already knew, Clark felt a wave of frustration ripple through him. Sometimes, being possessed of superhuman powers was a lot more trouble than it was worth. For a start, it meant there was a permanent barrier between him and his friends. However well they thought they knew him, there was a large part of him they could never know. A part he had to take deliberate efforts to conceal from them.

No matter where he went, or how relaxed the company, Clark always had to beware of letting his guard slip, of allowing anyone else to enter the strange parallel world he really inhabited.

After all, he was an alien—from where, and why, he would probably never know. But that didn't stop him thinking about it. He loved his adoptive parents more than anything in the world, but still he found himself wondering about his real parents, his real home.

Why had he be sent on his mysterious journey? What had happened to the world he'd been exiled from?

These were questions he couldn't answer.

"Kent, you're daydreaming again." Mrs. Bartsen's brusque tone jerked him out of his reverie. "Perhaps you'll wake up if you stand and explain to your peers the rudiments of n-dimensional superstring theory."

Clark smiled inwardly as he rose to his feet. This, at least, was a question he *could* answer.

CHAPTER 2

Monday afternoon

At lunch break, all anybody could talk about was the forth-coming party at Lex Luthor's castle. Originally standing on a windswept Scottish cliff, the entire structure had been dismantled stone by stone, shipped to the U.S., and rebuilt on a tree-studded estate on the outskirts of town.

It was supposed to have been the Smallville home of Lionel Luthor, billionaire boss of LuthorCorp and owner of the town's fertilizer plant. For despite his promises to the Ross brothers, Luthor had gone ahead and closed the creamed corn factory anyway. Now the building had been converted into the most advanced fertilizer production plant in Kansas.

And Lionel never bothered even to visit.

Instead, he'd sent his twenty-one-year-old son Lex to head up the plant. Or into exile, depending on whose side of the story you heard.

Now, to mark his first anniversary as a Smallville resident, Lex had announced he'd be hosting a weekend party for the town's teenagers.

"Invites are like gold dust," Chloe said, sharing a table with Clark and Pete in the school cafeteria.

"Guess I'll be passing up on mine," Pete said miserably. "Because there's no way Dad will let me go. He still hates LuthorCorp for reneging on their promises when he sold the factory." He rolled his eyes. "Whole family hates anything to do with the name Luthor, in fact."

"Your dad won't mind," Clark insisted. "It's a party. You just need to pick the right time to ask. Nobody can hold a grudge forever."

"Man, you don't know my family! We've been here since 1870. We don't forget anything, believe me!"

The youngest of eight, Pete felt overshadowed in almost everything he ever did by the triumphs of his high-achieving brothers and sisters. Sometimes, he felt that the others had already done everything there was to do, won every prize and honor that could be won, leaving the runt of the litter to bask in their reflected glory.

"I can feel it in my bones, guys. There'll be no party for Peter Ross!"

Clark was about to reply, seeking the words that would cheer up his friend, when out of the corner of his eye he caught sight of Lana's trim figure heading for their table.

"Room for one more?" she asked, indicating the vacant space.

"Always room for you, Lana," Pete told her, glancing pointedly at Clark.

Lana sat down opposite Clark, who immediately felt mild nausea sweep over him. Swallowing hard, he sat back slightly, trying to place just a little more distance between himself and that shiny, green-stone necklace.

"Everybody going to Lex's party Saturday?" Lana asked brightly. Only Pete shook his head, and groaned. "I wondered if maybe one of you could give me a little advice . . . ?"

"Sure," Chloe said beneath her breath, but just loudly enough for Clark to hear. "Dump Whitney and go with Clark to the party."

Clark's cheeks flushed red. "What kind of advice, Lana?" he asked, though as soon as she replied he wished he'd kept silent.

"I want to buy a gift for Whitney. Something out of the ordinary. You know, something special for the party."

"Isn't there anything in town he might like?" Chloe wanted to know. "Or does Golden Boy already own everything Smallville has for sale?"

"Oh, you know what it's like." Lana shrugged expressively. "Boyfriends!"

Clark felt a stab of sympathy for Chloe. She didn't know what it was like. She hadn't had a proper boyfriend since she'd arrived here from Metropolis. Clark knew that Pete really liked her, but she treated him as a good friend, nothing else. *Just like Lana and me.*

"Looks like a trip to the Big Met," Clark suggested. "Don't know when you'll make it, though—we have four full days of school before the weekend, and Mr. Tait's philosophy paper is due in by the end of the week."

"Yikes!" Chloe shot to her feet. "I forgot all about that. See you later, guys. The library calls."

"Like she's going to fail philosophy," Pete remarked, as Chloe headed for the exit. He looked thoughtful for a moment, then went on: "My folks sometimes buy gifts from a little place on—Durban Street, I think it is."

Lana's eyebrows furrowed. "Is there a shop on Durban? It's a little off the beaten track. I can't remember the last time I was over that way."

"There certainly used to be a place," Clark agreed. "My dad once bought something for my mom there. It's a long time since I heard them mention it, though. It's owned by an old lady, Miss Mayfern, I think."

"Great," Lana said enthusiastically, sweeping her books up under her arm. "I'll head up there after school." She stood up. "Anyone fancy keeping me company? Clark?"

Clark groaned to himself. There was nothing he'd rather do than be with Lana—even if it meant helping choose a gift

for her boyfriend. "I can't," he said ruefully. "I promised
Dad I'd put in a couple of hours on the farm when I get
home tonight."

He knew that Lana understood. Though Nell owned a big
house and lived a life of comparative leisure, many of their
neighbors were small farmers. She knew how much hard
work, how much sheer, unrelenting effort, went into keeping
small farms going in a world where "bigger" had somehow
come to mean "better."

"See you in class then." Lana waved her farewell. "Mr.
Tait next—last lesson before the paper's due. So I hope
you're not overloading your systems with too many stimu-
lants."

Pete started, and looked guiltily at his third soda. "Maybe
the girl has a point," he admitted.

But Clark was barely listening. He was watching Lana as
she walked toward the exit. So graceful. So pretty.

So out of his reach.

Midafternoon found Jonathan Kent out on the perimeter
of his east fields, on the banks of the stream that bordered
the farm. He was stripped to the waist, wielding a seven-
pound sledgehammer with a smooth ease born of long years
of practice. Time and again, the hammerhead rose up, then
swung down to strike the cap-protector on the fence post.
With each swing, the post sank inches farther into the
ground.

The sun shone from a cloudless, powder blue sky. It was
hot on his back, and Jonathan perspired freely. Despite his
making it look so simple, fencing work could never be
called easy. He'd been meaning to fix this section for a couple of weeks, since a storm had brought down a major limb

from a spreading willow tree, smashing a good twenty feet of fencing below.

Of course, he could have asked Clark, and the boy would have done it in a minute. Literally. Combining his colossal strength with his incredible speed and eye for detail, Clark could probably replace the entire border wire in just a few hours.

But there were some things Jonathan liked to keep for himself. He'd been used to hard manual labor all his life, first as a farmer's son, then as his inheritor. He loved the outdoor life and could never have lived any other.

"Ahh . . ."

Over his own labored breathing, Jonathan heard a sound halfway between a cough and a greeting. He lowered the hammer carefully and turned toward the noise.

A skinny man dressed in a dusty black motorcycle jacket and denim jeans stood about twenty feet away, just off the dirt track. He had a bulky travel bag slung over one shoulder. His black hair was thinning rapidly, and the pallor of his face seemed somehow unhealthy. Jonathan felt he recognized him from someplace, but couldn't quite put his finger on where.

"How can I help you?" Jonathan asked.

He could see no sign of a vehicle. If the man had walked out from town, it was no wonder he was coated in a fine layer of dust.

"I stepped down from the train when it slowed for the signal." The stranger nodded vaguely away across the fields toward the distant railroad track that connected Smallville with the big city, a three-hour ride away. "I'm heading for Smallville."

"Then you got off too soon. You have a fair walk from here."

"Thing is . . ." The man hesitated. His eyes kept engaging

Jonathan's, then sliding away. Not exactly furtive. Careful. As if he wasn't used to dealing with people. Or maybe, Jonathan realized, he was used to dealing with the wrong sort of people. "Thing is, I've just moved here from the city. I'm looking for a job."

Jonathan laughed.

"I'm a good worker," the man said quickly.

"I don't doubt it. But that's not why I laughed. You've come to the wrong place, is all." Jonathan waved a hand at the farmland surrounding them. "This farm needs three to run it, but it only pays enough for one salary. Me and my wife and son manage pretty well between us."

He saw disappointment in the newcomer's eyes. "I was kind of hoping . . ."

"I don't mean to break bad news," Jonathan went on, "but I think you'll find the answer is the same on every farm. Most folks are struggling to get by. Only ones making a profit are the big conglomerates—and they have machinery to do the work of men." He paused thoughtfully, studying the stranger. "Are you from around these parts? You seem sort of familiar to me."

"I lived in Smallville once. About a dozen years ago."

Jonathan suddenly knew why he recognized the man. Twelve years ago, his photograph had been on the front page of every newspaper in the state. Though Jonathan had never known him personally, the case had involved friends of his. "I thought I knew your face. You're Ray Dansk."

"Yes. I am." Dansk paused, his jaw jutting forward aggressively. "What of it?"

"Nothing of it. Just thought I recognized you, is all." He didn't add: the man who killed Bill Abbot.

"That why you won't give me a job—because of what I did?" Dansk demanded hotly. Jonathan started to shake his head, but Dansk rushed on without waiting for him to reply.

"Sir, I killed that guy. I didn't mean it, but I never tried to deny it. I've done my time. I've paid my debt." His eyes slid groundward again, and the anger faded from his voice. "Now I just want to find a job, settle down, and get on with my life."

"I respect that, Mr. Dansk," Jonathan said quietly. "If I had a job to offer, my answer might be different. But believe me, there is no work in small-scale farming."

The corner of Dansk's mouth twitched down, giving his pallid face a sudden hangdog look. He took a pack of cigarettes from his pocket, flipped the lid, and stuck one in his mouth. He fired it with a match. Without saying another word, he started walking back toward the track.

"If you're serious," Jonathan called after him on impulse, "try the LuthorCorp fertilizer plant. They sometimes take on casual workers."

Dansk stopped and looked back over his shoulder. "Fertilizer plant?" he repeated blankly.

"Over at the old Ross place," Jonathan told him. "You won't recognize it. There have been a lot of changes around here since you . . . went away."

"Yeah, I saw the housing developments off the train. Quarter of a million for a house in Smallville." He shook his head almost sadly. "Man, it's a different world."

Jonathan stood leaning on his hammer, watching as Dansk regained the track and started to walk away. Yes, there certainly had been a lot of changes in the past twelve years—and not all of them for the good.

Jonathan just hoped Ray Dansk's return didn't mark another turn for the worse. Memories lingered for a long time in a small town. Folk didn't forget easily, especially not the death of someone they cared for.

And Bill Abbot's family still lived in town.

Jonathan shrugged. He walked over to the stream, and

took out a bottle of water from where it was cooling. He drank deep, and replaced the bottle.

Then he picked up his hammer and began to swing.

"So, Miss Lang, can we hear your interpretation of what Plato was saying?"

Henry Tait stood ramrod stiff in front of the class, all of whom also sat unusually straight at their desks. Henry Tait allowed nobody, least of all himself, to slouch. It was thirty years since he'd seen combat duty in Vietnam, but he still exercised for an hour every morning and night. And he still adopted the posture—in fact, it had become part of him. Henry Tait's shoulders couldn't droop if he wanted them to.

Lana glanced down at the sheaf of notes on the desktop in front of her. Tait knew that philosophy was far from her favorite subject, but Lana was a good student and tried very hard.

"If I've picked him up correctly," Lana began, "Plato seems to be saying that people—all human life, in fact—is just some kind of illusion. A reflection, somehow, of a perfect world that seems to exist in a dimension we can be aware of but will always be inferior to."

Tait raised a finger to his lips, thoughtfully brushing the small, dark mustache above them. "And how do *you* feel about that, Miss Lang?"

Lana looked confused. "I guess I've never really thought about it," she admitted. "I mean, it's just another philosophy, isn't it? One among hundreds. Thousands."

Tait nodded, casting his eyes over the rest of the class. If they weren't paying attention, at least they were working hard pretending to. All except Clark Kent. His body faced forward, but his head was tilted to the side. For a better view of Lana Lang, three rows away, Tait decided.

"Let's think about it now," the teacher went on. "Because, believe it or not, much of Plato's philosophy is the foundation of politics today." He paused, and flicked a light sheen of chalk dust from the sleeve of his jacket. "Mr. Kent? Is it all right with you if we discuss this?"

Clark hadn't listened to a word since class began. He was lost in a daydream, stepping from a limo with Lana on his arm. Hand in hand, they made their way along red-carpeted halls to a stately ballroom, where the dancing spontaneously stopped as the revelers moved back to watch the golden couple. Resplendent in his tuxedo and black tie, Clark swept Lana into his arms and took to the dance floor. Rainbow light from a crystal chandelier played over them as they spun around the floor.

But the daydream deflated as Mr. Tait addressed him, and Clark gave a guilty start. He was conscious that, next to him, Pete Ross was grinning broadly at his friend's discomfiture.

"Yes, Mr. Tait," Clark said, though he hadn't a clue what they were going to discuss. "Of course, sir."

After the war had ended, Henry Tait returned to his parents' home in Metropolis and enrolled in college on the G.I. Bill. Long before he ever graduated, though, he knew that city life was no longer for him. After what he'd seen in Asia—and, some whispered, what he'd done there—he knew that his life required a drastic change.

Initially in an effort to understand the two years of hell he'd lived through, he immersed himself in philosophy. Gradually it came to fascinate him, and when he got his teaching diploma he deliberately decided to apply for a job in the smallest, most isolated town that would have him.

Smallville High won out by a mile.

"Basically," the teacher said now, "Miss Lang is right. Plato is telling us we're not real, we don't matter. Somehow, greater beings, greater events, run our universe. That belief echoes down the centuries until today, more than two thousand years later, it's still in vogue. And in the opinion of some," he added, "that is precisely what is wrong with our world today. Nobody is willing to take responsibility. Why should they, when according to Plato all we can do is observe shadows on a cave wall? If there are superior beings—gods and goddesses, if you will—why should ordinary people take responsibility for themselves?"

Chloe Sullivan's hand shot in the air, and Tait nodded his permission for her to speak. "Are you suggesting, sir, that religion is responsible for the world's troubles?"

"Good question, Chloe." Tait nodded with satisfaction. Chloe had a quick, inquiring mind, and could be relied on to see straight to the heart of much that went over the heads of the others. "But no, that's not what I'm saying. Personally, I think religion is a matter of choice. But life"—his hand thumped down on his desktop, emphasizing his point—"is not a matter of choice. It is, perhaps, a gift. A gift for which each of us must bear our own responsibility.

"If we're beaten down, we must get up and plunge into the struggle again. If we suffer loss, we must grieve, then move on. If the world is going to hell in a hand basket . . ." The class could tell from his tone that he believed it was. ". . . then it is the responsibility of each of us to do something about it. Don't look to governments for your answers. Don't look to gurus, or astrologers, or authorities to guide you."

His voice dropped, as if he'd suddenly realized that this

degree of fervor might sound more religious than philosophical. "Look inside yourself. At the end of the day, when all is said and done, that's all you have. Your own self."

Chloe's hand was in the air again. "That doesn't exactly square with Plato's other ideas, does it, sir?" Tait was silent, waiting for her to continue. "I mean, he maintained that mankind was a savage, bloodthirsty species. He believed that, if left to our own devices, we'd eventually exterminate each other in an orgy of annihilation. He claimed that we needed an educated elite to rule the world, to save us from our bestial selves."

"Very insightful, Chloe." Henry Tait noted Chloe's small smile of satisfaction. Not only could the girl think, she liked to kick up a little controversy now and again. "And what does the class think? Have Plato's educated elites succeeded in their task?"

Again, it was Chloe who answered. "We only need to take a look at the world, sir, to realize they've *failed.* Abysmally. Violence is endemic to almost every human society. There hasn't been any period in the past two thousand years when there *wasn't* a war. It's almost as if, after the Golden Age of Reason, we're descending back into superstition and cult worship."

"Excellent, Chloe."

There was the sound of a bell from the corridor outside, and Henry Tait glanced at his watch. "Miss Sullivan's observations will form the basis of next week's class. Meanwhile, time—as the philosopher said—has overtaken us. You may go."

There was a clattering of seats being pushed back, and the sudden thrum of twenty voices talking all at once as his students gathered their belongings and made for the exit.

"Don't forget to hand in your papers on Friday," Tait announced to their departing backs. "Chloe, would you mind staying behind for a moment? I have a couple of books I'd like to recommend to you."

Clark Kent made to pass, but Tait blocked his way. "I'd like you to stay behind as well, Mr. Kent." Seeing Kent's quizzical look, he added: "You seem to spend most of my classes in a daydream. I'm going to set you some extra work, see if that will pique your interest."

He ignored Kent's groan and began to scribble down the information for Chloe.

Lex Luthor sat in his office at the fertilizer plant, sighing as he pored over the company's accounts for the past three months. Costs were down by nearly 20 percent, productivity was up by half that, and still his father was firing off memos demanding higher profitability.

The telephone buzzed and, glad of the distraction, Lex picked it up.

"There's a young lady here to see you," the receptionist told him. "She refuses to give her name—says she wants to surprise you."

Lex grinned. "Bring her right up, please, Anne. And could we have coffee for two? Black for me, cream and sugar for my guest."

Minutes later, there was a tap on his door. Anne, his receptionist, looked apologetic. But before she could speak, a woman in a black jacket and orange skirt pushed past her.

"Lex!" Lex got to his feet as she rushed forward and threw her arms around him. "Darling!"

Over her shoulder, Lex winked at Anne. "Thanks," he told her. "Don't forget the coffee."

"Renata," Lex responded to the woman's embrace, trying

not to be overwhelmed by her musky perfume. "How nice to see you. When did you get into town?"

"This morning. I didn't call because . . . well, I wanted it to be a surprise."

Lex pursed his lips, trying to hide his amusement. Renata Meissen looked as if she'd just stepped out of the pages of a fashion magazine—standard dress for Metropolis, perhaps, but rare in Smallville. One of Lex's many acquaintances had called him shortly after the train arrived, describing the newcomer. Lex knew immediately who she was.

He and Renata had enjoyed a brief but passionate fling some years back, when Lex was busy acquiring his playboy reputation in the city. He sometimes wondered if that was why his father had exiled him to Smallville—to hide his son from any consequences his wild behavior might have had.

"So . . . what brings you to this tiny corner of my father's empire?"

"The train, actually," Renata joked. "I felt a sudden urge to see the countryside."

"And what do you think of Smallville?"

Renata rolled her eyes. "It's like the last stop on the road to nowhere."

"For now, maybe," Lex said. His face was suddenly serious, and there was no trace of humor in his voice. "One day, I'll make it famous."

Anne came in with a tray of coffee, and Lex waited until she left before speaking again.

"The Renata Meissen I knew would have hired a chopper to get here."

Renata tossed her head, her long blond hair swinging back from her face like a curtain. "Times change." She shrugged. "I had a problem."

Lex knew all about that. The story of her addiction to

cocaine had been plastered over the society pages of every newspaper on the East Coast. "Did you solve it?"

"Six months in a Swiss clinic solved it." She smiled thinly. "Expensive, though. And of course, few companies want a recovering addict working for them. So . . ." She brightened suddenly. ". . . I thought I'd come see you for a while."

"Great."

Lex's mind was racing as he raised the coffee to his lips. Sure, he and Renata had a great time—while it lasted. But it was years in the past. He'd never thought of her since, and he'd be willing to bet she hadn't thought much about him, either.

If Renata Meissen had made the effort to get to the last stop on the road to nowhere, he knew she had a damn good reason.

CHAPTER 3

Monday evening

With a population of only 45,001, Smallville seemed to be doing all it could to justify its name. The population had nearly doubled in the past fifteen or so years, but it was still little more than a backwoods town in the middle of one of the country's least-populated states.

The center of town could almost have been lifted from the set of a 1950s movie. Main Street boasted a garage, a bank, the town's main hotel, the old cinema, restaurants, and shops. Numerous small streets ran off the main square, many of them lined with century-old town houses set back from the street behind majestic plane and lime trees. Descendants of the original owners still lived in a surprising number of the weather-boarded homes.

Durban Street was a quiet lane that sloped up to the bluff overlooking the Smallville River. The houses there had seen better days, and the majority of them would have benefited from a general scrubdown and paint job.

Lana Lang had headed here after school was over. Aunt Nell was hosting a bridge afternoon for some of her cronies out at the house, and agreed to pick her up later. For the past twelve years Nell had been both mother and father to Lana. Now she was a teenager, so Nell was also having to learn the role of big sister.

It was a long time since Lana had been in this part of town. Her eyes roved everywhere as she walked slowly up the incline, taking in long-forgotten sights. The Spanish chestnut tree in front of the old Payne place was still there, and Lana couldn't help smiling when she saw it. When she was five or six, she'd been best friends with Beth-Ann Payne. She'd spent a lot of time playing here as Nell struggled to come to terms with her new role in life.

She paused to gaze up into the leafy branches, remembering the swing Beth-Ann's dad had fixed up for them one long and glorious summer. *Must have been the year before Mr. Payne lost his job,* Lana thought with a twinge of sadness. Like so many others had done, the Payne family relocated to Metropolis. Lana and Beth-Ann had kept in touch for a while, but kids aren't great letter writers. Now the ritual exchange of Christmas cards each year was their only contact.

Funny how the past has a habit of slipping through your fingers. And the harder you try to hold on to it, the faster it slips away.

The street was deserted, except for one man in a black biker's jacket on the other side. He was walking down the hill toward town, eyes downcast, sweeping the ground. Lana didn't recognize him, and he seemed not to even notice her.

At the end of the street, the paved road turned into a hard-packed gravel track. Miss Mayfern's house stood off to the side, almost perched right on top of the fifty-foot bluff. The view from her garden, looking over the meandering river below, meant it wouldn't be long before the developers were sniffing around this part of town.

Lana could barely remember the house, let alone its ever having been a shop. But a small wooden sign, its paint blistered and peeling from long exposure to the Kansas sun, was hammered into the edge of the sprawling, unkempt lawn. MISS MAYFERN'S SPECIAL GIFTS, Lana read. Though, if the sign was anything to go by, it might have been years since the shop had actually traded. Lana couldn't figure how an old lady could possibly make a living in this out-of-the-way corner.

She turned off the track and walked up the path toward the faded Gothic house. Weeds poked out from between the flagstones. A wooden staircase led up to the front door, whose peeling paint and cracked glass cried out for renovation. In a Metropolis suburb, a house like this would be worth a considerable sum of money. In Smallville, it was worth hardly anything . . . at least until the developers showed an interest.

As she was about to ascend the stairs, Lana saw another sign, almost obscured by several briars that had wound themselves around it. It was a simple arrow pointing to the side of the house, where a set of steps led down to the basement. Hardly daring to believe the shop would still be open, Lana followed the sign past an old-fashioned well at the side of the overgrown lawn.

At the bottom of the steps was a half-glass door, with so much dust on the panes that Lana couldn't even see inside. Convinced she was here on a wild-goose chase, Lana reached for the brass door handle and was surprised when it turned easily in her hand.

A bell rang as she pushed open the door and entered the tiny shop, a room carved out of one end of the house's basement.

The shop looked as if it had been destocked forty years earlier, then abandoned. A ragged tailor's dummy stood just inside the doorway, wearing a delicate lace scarf disfigured by years of dust. A half barrel stood in the center of the floor, under a sign that said LUCKY DIP 2 CENTS. Lana peered in, wondering what she'd get for two cents these days, but the barrel was completely empty. The shelves tacked to the dirty cream-colored walls were practically bare, though here and there Lana could see small ornaments and books that remained unsold.

There was a tiny sales counter, and from the doorway behind it, Lana heard the sound of slowly approaching feet.

"Miss Mayfern?" she asked, as the door pushed open and a frail-looking old lady entered.

She squinted up at Lana, her piercing blue eyes almost invisible in the crow's-feet that surrounded them. When she spoke, her voice was surprisingly strong and lucid. "Yes, that's me," she said, the words crisp, almost staccato. "Who wants to know?"

Lana introduced herself, and Miss Mayfern nodded her head vigorously. "Knew your folks. A real asset to this town." Her eyes glazed over, and for a moment Lana thought the old lady was going to lose herself in ancient memories. But almost at once she went on. "They're sorely missed. Remember you well, too. Pretty child." She took a step back and scrutinized the teenager. "Grown up pretty, too. A lot don't, you know."

Lana flushed slightly at the compliment. "Thank you," she said graciously. "I want to buy a gift for my boyfriend, and someone suggested you. But"—she glanced around, as if to confirm her earlier impression—"I guess you're not open anymore."

"Then you guess wrong," Miss Mayfern said snappily. "I opened this shop in 1951. You ever see it closed, means I'm dead."

Lana quickly apologized. "I didn't mean to offend you. It's just . . . I don't see very much stock."

"Don't see too many customers these days," Miss Mayfern admitted grudgingly. "So I don't need to carry a lot." She uncurled a bony finger and tapped the side of her nose, as if she was letting Lana in on some deep secret. "But I still have some nice things."

I wonder where? Lana thought. Some of the items on the shelves might have been special three or four decades ago, but there was nothing she'd seen that was remotely suitable for Whitney. She was trying to think of an excuse for leaving when Miss Mayfern preempted her, pointing to a pair of dusty cane chairs next to a small table.

"Sit," the old lady said authoritatively. She shuffled back out the door through which she'd entered. "We'll have a cup of mint tea, while you tell me all about yourself."

Lana felt unable to disobey. It would be rude to leave Miss Mayfern now, and besides, it would do no harm to while away half an hour or so on a balmy evening. She sat down in the chair, its thin cushion puffing out a small nebula of dust that swirled and drifted in the shafts of honeyed sunlight pouring through the basement window.

Miss Mayfern returned a few minutes later, carrying two glasses of iced mint tea. She handed one to Lana, then seated herself on the chair facing her.

"Who is the gift for?" she asked brusquely.

Lana took a sip of her cool green drink, her mouth tingling slightly at the fresh, clean taste of mint. "Whitney. Whitney Fordman, my boyfriend," Lana replied, feeling strangely shy. The old lady's keen blue eyes had never left hers, making Lana just slightly uncomfortable. "He's captain of the football team. We're going to a big party Saturday night, at the Luthor mansion. I want something special for Whitney to remember it by."

"Do you love him?"

The directness of the question took Lana by surprise. "I . . . I . . ."she faltered. It was something she'd asked herself a hundred times. She enjoyed being with Whitney. She could rely on him, and he made her feel safe, and secure. But was that love?

"Don't know, do you?" Miss Mayfern gave a short, low-pitched laugh, the sound incongruous coming from her frail, birdlike figure. "Always best to know, that's my advice." Her eyes took on that faraway look again, and there was a long silence before she resumed speaking. "Didn't know myself, once. Didn't know till it was too late. And life only offered me the one chance of happiness."

"What happened?" Lana asked, feeling like an intruder in the old lady's memories.

"War happened. He was drafted. Killed in Germany, 1945."

"I'm sorry," Lana said softly, genuinely feeling for the old lady's loss.

Miss Mayfern went on as if Lana hadn't spoken. "I was fourteen. Not much younger than you. Alick was eighteen. Wanted me to say I loved him before he left. I couldn't. I didn't know. By the time I decided, it was too late." She sighed, took a sip of her tea, and seemed to disappear in the mists of her mind.

Lana wracked her brains, desperate to turn the tide of the depressing conversation. Miss Mayfern made her discomfort unnecessary.

"Any other boyfriends?" she demanded.

"No, not really. Whitney and I have been going out for a year." Lana drank deep from her glass. The tea was ice-cold, but somehow it seemed to spread a warm glow through her. She gave a little laugh. "There's a boy in my class who likes me. He's nice, but . . . well, he's the same age as me. Not nearly as mature as Whitney."

"Mature isn't important. Happiness is important." The old lady's eyes seemed to be staring right through her. "Maybe the only thing that is. They won't teach you that in school."

Lana was growing used to Miss Mayfern's peculiar way

of talking. She was direct, and to the point, eschewing banalities and trivia.

"What's his name, this immature boy?"

"Clark. Clark Kent. His parents own the farm next to my aunt's place."

Miss Mayfern nodded knowingly. "Good folks. Jonathan bought Martha a gift here once," she crowed. "Rainbow brooch. Paste jewels, of course. But goodness, did it sparkle in the sunlight!" Abruptly, she changed the subject. "Whitney makes you feel safe. Why is that important to you?"

That was something Lana had never really asked herself. She just liked the way Whitney was so protective of her—as if, no matter what life might throw at them, he had strength enough to handle it for both of them. She must have taken too long thinking it over, she realized, because Miss Mayfern was talking again.

"I'll tell you why. Your parents." Those blue eyes stared into Lana's, as if they could see all the way into her very soul. "They died. You were only three. You didn't understand. Thought they'd abandoned you. Cried yourself to sleep at nights, wondering why they never came back."

Lana felt tears prick her eyes. "How . . . how do you know that?"

Miss Mayfern reached to lift the pitcher and refilled both their glasses. "I'm seventy years old, Lana," she said, an enigmatic smile on her face. "What I don't know, I can guess at." She handed Lana her glass, the swirling green liquid seeming to glow with an inner light.

"Now drink your tea, and we'll see about this special gift."

✦✦✦

The shadows were lengthening, the sun sinking fast in the clear sky. On Main Street the store lights were already ablaze, and the streetlamps would soon follow.

Ray Dansk paid the cashier at the Beanery, and headed out into the gathering twilight. He paused in the doorway to light a cigarette, gulping the smoke greedily into his lungs.

He felt exhausted, barely refreshed by the burger and two portions of fries he'd just wolfed down. He must have walked for miles today, from farm to farm to stinking farm. The guy fixing the fence had been right. He stood more chance of striking gold than finding work in Smallville. Same story at the fertilizer plant—some geek in a white coat looking down his nose and telling Ray there was nothing for a month. At least.

He'd cheered up when he saw the STACKERS WANTED sign in the window of a small supermarket. Wasn't much, but it would be a start. Give him a base to operate from, enough to rent a room at least and start to put his life back together again.

Just his luck, though. They were looking for teenagers, high-school students who'd work for a fraction of what a man needed to get by. He'd come close to a public shouting match with the store owner, but thought better of it, shrugged, and walked out.

Still didn't make any sense to him, though. They had work, he wanted work. Equation's as simple as that. What was it they used to say in the pen? "Life's a bitch . . . and then you die."

No point thinking that way. There was a lot of life in Ray Dansk yet.

He jammed his hands into his jacket pockets and hunched his shoulders against the cool breeze that was springing up now day was done. The welfare office would be closed, so he'd get no help there. He didn't have enough left from his liberty cash to stay in the hotel. Not if he wanted to eat, anyway. Where the hell was he going to sleep tonight?

He'd asked around for his old buddies, Laker and Judd. The first few folk he'd met didn't have a clue. He checked their old stomping grounds, everywhere the guys might be hanging out. He could move in with one of them till he found work.

But the dingy bar whose name he couldn't even remember was gone, replaced by a chic new computer games outlet. He'd even got lost once, heading for Riverside Park, where the Dragons used to race along the path that ran parallel to the riverbank. He ended up on Durban Street, on top of the bluff instead of below it.

It was the mechanic at the garage who told him. Laker had signed up for the army nearly ten years ago. Judd had heeded the siren call of the city and headed for the bright lights of Metropolis. Smallville never heard of either of them again.

Makes sense. No family, no work. What was the point in hanging out in World's End?

World's End . . . that's what they used to call it, the three of them, back in the days when they were full of fire. The Dragons, Smallville's own motorcycle gang. Dansk smiled thinly to himself. Those were the days when they'd thought they were something. When nothing could touch them. And the future—in some never-defined way—was whatever they wanted.

They'd race their modified motorcycles for hours on end. If the weather was bad, and they had no cash, they would hole out in the caves at the foot of the bluff. They'd build a fire and sit around it, smoking and popping cans of beer, staring into the flames and dreaming of the big shots they'd become. One day.

I hope Laker and Judd made it.

But he doubted it.

He realized he was standing outside the Talon cinema, all boarded up and abandoned now. He'd spent a large part of his teenage years in its comforting darkness, watching his idols on the big screen. Arnie. Sly. The European kickboxer with the foreign name.

Maybe he could find a way in, sleep there for the night, and start afresh tomorrow.

But the door was solidly padlocked, and there were bars on the windows. He briefly toyed with the idea of going around the back, maybe breaking in where he was unlikely to be seen. But he dismissed the notion as soon as it came to him. Okay, maybe World's End was a bummer. But if he was caught breaking and entering, they'd have him right back in the pen.

Dansk cursed, and set out to retrace his steps. Going straight wasn't proving to be as easy as he'd assumed.

The lights of the Beanery shone welcomingly ahead. After twelve years of prison slop, the burgers were like manna.

And maybe the coffee would get his mind working on someplace to stay.

Darkness had fallen by the time Lana left Miss Mayfern's basement.

Walking down Durban toward where she'd asked Aunt Nell to meet her, she felt both elated and strangely detached. Behind her crusty facade, the old lady had a heart of gold. They'd talked for simply ages, the conversation ranging wildly from wars and economic depression to what made men sexy.

Lana couldn't remember the half of what they'd said. She'd felt so at ease, the same way she did with her aunt, as if she'd known the old lady for years and years. As if they shared some deep bond.

Aunt Nell was waiting in the rapidly emptying parking lot off the central square, standing next to her Grand Cherokee. She smoothed back her chestnut hair with her hand to allow Lana to plant a kiss on her cheek. She snapped the button on her key ring, and the doors unlocked.

"You look happy," Nell remarked, as they clambered into the vehicle.

"Mmm," Lana replied dreamily. "Miss Mayfern is one nice lady."

"It's a long time since I've seen her." Nell inserted her key in the car ignition, but didn't start the engine. "So . . . ?" she asked.

Lana stared blankly at her.

"What did you buy?" Nell prompted. "Remember—you went to buy a gift?"

"Oh. Yes. Of course." Lana laughed, as if she just remembered herself why she'd gone there. "What do you think of this?"

She pulled a wedge of tissue paper from her pocket. Nell leaned over as she carefully unwrapped it, to reveal a tiny silver star tiepin. Each of its points was about a quarter inch long.

"It's exquisite, Lana. Whitney's going to adore it."

"Whitney?" Lana's brows furrowed. "It's not for Whitney."

Lana held the little tiepin up between thumb and forefinger. It twirled in her hand, reflecting the orange glow of a streetlamp a few yards away.

"It's for Clark."

◆◆◆

The pale moon cast pale shadows as Ray Dansk made his way along the path in Riverside Park. A few yards to his side, the Smallville River splashed and gurgled as it tumbled in its rocky bed. Moonlight shimmered on its surface.

The idea had come to him as he'd drunk his third cup of coffee. It was obvious he wasn't going to find accommodation for the night, and there was no point seeking work before morning. He played with the idea of going to a bar or tavern and sinking a few beers, but discounted it. He'd never been a heavy drinker, and twelve years without a taste didn't really faze him.

And then he'd remembered the cave.

There was nobody in the park at this hour, though the mushroom lights that picked out the path and picnic area still burned. Dansk followed them to the end of the park, where the path looped back on itself in a circular walk. A wire fence marked the boundary. Dansk stooped to slip through the top strands, and seconds later was moving through the long grass and scrubby bushes on the other side.

The dark mass of the bluff loomed above him as he squinted his eyes, trying to follow the faint path that had once cut through the overgrown brush. He ignored the red-painted DANGER KEEP OUT! sign hammered into the ground and made his way toward the entrance of the small cave that ran back into the base of the bluff.

The entrance was boarded up—it always had been—and in the moonlight he could make out a few initials and names that Smallville teenagers had carved on the wooden planks. His own name, and Laker's and Judd's, had once been scrawled there.

The caves had been a popular draw with the town's young folk for years. Despite the potential dangers, and the efforts of the authorities to keep people away, the area was like a magnet to teenagers with not enough money and too much time.

The boards had been replaced at least once since Dansk was last here. They were heavier than he remembered, held in place with iron hoops nailed flush to the wood. But there was a slight depression in the ground under the lowest board. He knelt down and used his hands to scoop away earth and stones, until the depression was just deep enough to allow him to lie down and crawl beneath.

Dansk held his breath and listened for a moment. Silence.

He stooped low and scrambled under the boards, cursing as his jacket snagged on a splinter of wood and almost ripped. Then he was inside, in the cool darkness. A few shafts of moonlight penetrated the interior, shining in through cracks and knotholes in the boards.

The cave ran back for about fifty feet, narrowing as it disappeared into pitch-blackness. Dansk fumbled in his pocket for his matches and sparked one into life. In the small glow cast by the flickering flame, he saw that the floor was strewn with litter—soda cans and candy wrappers, cigarette butts and fading newspapers. Water trickled here and there from the cave roof, dribbling down the walls, forming little pools on the uneven floor. Near the entrance, the walls and floor were covered in thick moss.

It was obvious nobody had been here in months.

Carefully, he picked a path through the trash, heading deeper into the cave. The rock walls angled closer together the farther he went, until finally the cave ended at a sheer wall. There was no litter here—trespassers usually stayed close to the entrance, and few ventured this deep into the recess.

Dansk struck another match, and moved back five or six feet. Just above head height he found what he was looking for. He could make out the contours of a rough hole in the cave wall.

He killed the match and reached up to grip the bottom of the hole. His feet scrambled for purchase on the smooth wall as he hauled himself up into the darkness. He cursed again as he struck his shoulder on a protrusion of rock, but then he was out into clear space. He lit another match. *Best go careful. Only half a book left.*

The guttering flame revealed that he was in another cave, little more than a pocket in the rock, about seven feet square and six feet high. Water oozed down the walls to pool on the cavern floor, but it was slightly drier than the main cave, and there was no litter at all.

Ray Dansk knew it well. This was where he'd hidden out after that terrible night, when he and Bill Abbott fought, and Abbott died. He'd stayed here for two days straight, terrified of what he'd done, but even more afraid of the punishment he would have to face for it.

In the end, cold and hungry and with no place else to go, Dansk had left the cave and surrendered himself at the Lowell County Sheriff's Office.

Now, twelve years later, he was back.

He smiled ruefully as he wedged his back against the cave wall, away from the dripping water, and stretched out his legs. Ironic that he should find himself here again, after all his determination to build himself a better life when he got out of jail.

He unwrapped one of several candy bars he'd bought, and gnawed at the chocolate without even tasting it. His eyelids were drooping, and he couldn't stop yawning. He must have walked twenty miles today, and his calves and thighs ached.

Better luck tomorrow, he promised himself. He tossed the candy wrapper aside and lit up a last cigarette. When it was done, he stubbed the butt out in a pool, closed his eyes, and fell at once into a deep sleep.

He didn't feel the drip of water that spattered onto his shoulder a few minutes later. If he'd still been awake—if he'd lit a precious match—he would have seen the strange green light that seemed to roil and twist in the droplet as it splashed on him.

Almost a minute later, another drip fell from the same place.

Within an hour, the sleeping man's shoulder and front were pooled with damp, and a tiny trickle, so small he didn't even feel it, was curling down inside his jacket . . .

Running over the fearsome dragon tattoo on his chest.

CHAPTER 4

Monday night

Outside town, the cornfields lay bathed in moonlight.

Up on the first floor platform of the old wooden barn, Clark Kent closed one eye and leaned closer to the viewfinder on the powerful telescope his father had given him.

The telescope barrel was slanted up and to the side, away from the area of sky where moonlight blotted out the twinkling stars. Several pinpricks of light squiggled in the eyepiece, and Clark patiently adjusted the focusing screws until the stars sprang sharply into relief. Orion's Belt, the near-straight line of three stars that bisected the constellation of the Hunter.

In actual fact, as Clark well knew, they bore absolutely no relation to each other except random chance. But viewed from Earth, they seemed to form a line in the same plane.

Clark adjusted the focus again, zeroing in on Betelgeuse, the giant red star. It glittered like a ruby against the velvet backdrop of space, and for the hundredth time Clark found himself wondering if it had a planetary system. A *viable* planetary system, he corrected himself, because Betelgeuse was a sun that had expanded to massive size and would probably have swallowed up any planets that orbited the star.

Astronomy was his favorite hobby, and he spent many nights up in this den his father had built him in the barn loft. He knew that more than a dozen solar systems had been observed out there in the heavens, their planets invisible to even the most powerful telescopes, but detectable by the gravitational forces that caused minute perturbations to the orbits of their central stars.

Could that be it? Clark wondered. *Could that be where I come from?*

Ever since his parents had revealed the truth about his origins, he'd been obsessed with scanning the night skies. They'd told him from an early age that he was adopted, and for many years the growing boy had accepted that without question. It was only when his remarkable powers started to reveal themselves that Jonathan and Martha had felt obliged to divulge the deeper truth.

Clark Kent was indeed adopted—but he was the son of no Earthly parents. The meteors that hit Smallville all those years ago had brought something other than weird green rocks to Earth. Hidden in the center of the sinuous swarm had been a tiny metallic spacecraft. That was what had landed in Jonathan's field that fateful day.

They'd told Clark all about it, how he'd been found wandering close to where the gleaming craft still lay in the smoking crater it had formed on impact. He'd shown no sign of injury. When he saw Martha and Jonathan hanging upside down in their wrecked vehicle, he reached in through the window to take Martha's hand, as if it was the most natural thing in the world.

As if, after an unknown time in cold, bleak space, the child was desperate for contact with another conscious being.

Now, the spacecraft was hidden away in a storm cellar close to the Kent farm. Jonathan had taken Clark to see it when he was fourteen years old. Marveling, Clark had laid his hand on the strange metal that was neither hot nor cold to the touch. He'd stayed there for hours, desperately hoping

that contact with the craft that had brought him to Earth
would tell him the truth about where he'd come from.

It hadn't.

The Kents had officially adopted him, claiming they
never knew the identity of his biological parents. Nobody
had ever questioned the reality of that, and as far as Clark
and his parents were concerned, nobody ever would. Alien
or not, adopted or not, the Kents loved Clark with all their
hearts. And he loved them.

To all intents and purposes, they *were* his parents.

But there would always be a part of him that needed to
pierce the mystery that lay at the core of his being.

Who was he, really? Who were his parents, on what
planet did they live, orbiting which sun? He'd speculated
that maybe it was a red giant, or a blue dwarf, even a black
hole, because his superpowers seemed to be directly connected to Earth's yellow sun. He felt best in summer,
slightly less strong in spring and autumn, and at his weakest
during the winter months.

Why had these unknown people entrusted their child to
an unmanned spacecraft and sent it hurtling through trillions
of miles of darkness, targeted on Smallville, Kansas, U.S.A.,
Planet Earth?

Clark sighed as he shifted the telescope on its tripod,
aiming it at a nearby patch of sky where there were no bright
stars, only faint smudges of light that came from galaxies
unimaginable distances away. Was one of them his home, a
planet circling a star so distant that its light had taken millions of years to reach Earth?

But then, how could anyone cover that distance in a
spacecraft, even traveling at the speed of light?

He felt an unquenchable sadness. If he'd traveled so far,
then his parents, and their whole culture, had crumbled to
dust long ago.

He might be the last survivor of an entire race.

Sighing again, he flicked the safety cap over the lens and covered the telescope.

His footsteps echoed on the bare wooden boards as he walked across to the ladder leading down to ground level.

He should save his dreams for when he was asleep.

In his dream, Ray Dansk was a Smallville Dragon again.

It was the week before the meteors fell, when Smallville still boasted it was the creamed corn capital of Kansas. Dansk and Laker and Judd roared into town on their hogs, gunning the engines, doing wheelies up Main Street. They parked their bikes and headed for the bar, swaggering across the street like they owned it. With their slicked-back hair, dirty denims, and black leather jackets, they felt part of an American tradition that reached back to the end of the Second World War.

The biker gang.

When Smallville residents looked at them, they saw young men pretending to be tough, youths acting out a fantasy, wasting their lives. But when the Dragons looked at each other, they saw Marlon Brando and Lee Marvin and Hell's Angels.

The dream shifted.

He was leaving the bar, feeling like he'd had one beer too many. Too drunk to drive, Laker and Judd said their noisy farewells and headed back to their parents' apartments. But Dansk's folks were dead, killed in an auto accident the previous year, and he hated to go back to the cold and lonely basement he rented.

So Ray had hung around Main Street, singing drunken

rock and roll, smoking and throwing the odd insult at anybody who ventured too close.

"You're a no-good bum, Dansk," a voice was saying, "a waste of space. You'd be doing us all a favor if you left town."

Bill Abbott, assistant manager at the Smallville Bank, was on his way home from a meal with his wife. Dansk had lost his balance as they passed, and staggered into Abbott's wife. He tried to apologize, but Abbott just kept on ranting at him.

"It's scum like you that give Smallville a bad name. Wise up, you moron!"

Dansk had no idea of what he'd replied, but it must have been nasty, because Abbott suddenly took a swing at him. It was a clumsy punch, with little force behind it, but it caught Dansk's shoulder and spun him around. He bounced off the wall of a building and came back with his fists flailing.

Abbott grabbed him around the waist and they fell to the sidewalk, wrestling.

Abbott was far from being the physical type, but anger fueled his blows. Dansk was winded by a sudden punch to the midriff, and he collapsed facedown, groaning. Then Abbott was kneeling on his back, punching ineffectually at his arms and shoulders.

Somehow, Dansk managed to twist around. Abbott lost his balance and slipped. He fell forward, and his forehead cracked against the corner of the raised curb.

He heard Abbott's wife scream, and he sobered up immediately. Terrified of what he'd done, Dansk took to his heels. He ran to the cave, where he huddled trembling for two days before giving himself up.

The dream shifted.

He was on trial, standing in the dock before a sea of hostile faces. If Mrs. Abbott had been the only witness, he could have tried to lie his way out. It would have been his word against hers.

But three others had seen what happened. Henry Tait, English and philosophy teacher at Smallville High, had been out for a late-night run.

Man, what kind of nut goes out running at close to midnight?

The woman who owned the Talon Theatre—Nell Potter—was on her way home when she saw the scuffle develop. And Louis Verne, chef at the Smallville Hotel, saw Dansk running away.

That's how it happened in real life. That's how it happened in his dream.

But now the dream took another, more sinister turn.

Dansk was skulking in a strange green mist, whose tendrils curled around him like living things. He was waiting for someone. He might have been waiting forever. Didn't matter. He had all the time in the world, and more.

The blood coursing in his veins felt thick and sluggish. His skin was dry and scaly. Wonderingly, he raised a hand to his mouth—and felt his razor claws brush against gleaming fangs. Saliva trickled from the corner of his lips.

His jacket was open to the waist, and he wore no T-shirt underneath. His muscles rippled. He felt stronger than he ever had in his life before. The dragon tattoo emblazoned on his chest seemed to be coiling and uncoiling, flexing its long tail. Its fierce red eyes glared like lasers through the mist, burning with hatred.

He was a lizard-man. A human dragon.

A figure jogged toward him through the mist, and the dragon on his chest roared.

Dansk leaped forward, slashing with those razor claws, fangs ripping and biting at whatever they could find. The shadowy figure yelled in pain. It tried to fight back, but Dansk was a Dragon, a whirlwind of bloody violence.

The figure screamed, and the green mist abruptly turned to red.

He was standing over a dead body, ripped and bleeding as if it had been savaged by a pack of wolves. Scraps of flesh clung to his claws, and he could taste fresh blood in his mouth.

Human blood.

His rage for vengeance had subsided. With the tip of his boot, he turned the body over.

The cold, dead eyes of Henry Tait stared sightlessly up at him.

He woke up in darkness, shivering in a cold sweat.

The dream had been so real! He could still feel the dragon now, writhing and undulating across his chest, its eyes burning. But his skin—his hands—his teeth—all felt normal again.

His heart thumping as if it would explode, Dansk fished in his jacket pocket for a cigarette. The pack was empty. He'd smoked the last one before he fell asleep.

He shrugged and tossed the empty packet into the darkness.

Who cares?

He couldn't help thinking about the dream, reliving every moment. The unnatural power that surged through his body. The hurricane force of his blows. The sweet taste of blood.

The pleasure that flooded through him at the memory of murder.

Grimly, he shook his head, trying to banish the thoughts. Ray Dansk wasn't that kind of guy. He didn't want revenge on anyone. He just wanted to settle down.

But somewhere deep inside him, he knew that emotions

that should never have been disturbed were seeing the light of day.

He didn't notice the water that pattered from the ceiling above, soaking into his clothes and his skin.

The green inside it was almost fluorescent, curling like a living organism.

"Welcome to the Winter Olympics here in Salt Lake City!"

Clark Kent hauled himself easily up to the jump-off point. He strapped his skis to his feet, took one look at the curving jump, then thrust himself forward with all his strength.

He hit the upslope of the jump ramp at close to 150 miles an hour, and soared high into the air. Looking down, he could see the faces of the crowd, turned up to watch him. And there was Lana, wrapped in a pure white snowsuit, hands to her face in concern as she watched the man she loved.

"And it's a new world record for Clark Kent of Small-ville—more than four times the previous best!"

Then he and Lana were standing on the deck of a mountain chalet, the sky purple and gold and magnificent as the sun set behind the mountains.

He turned to her. Her eyes closed, and she raised her lips. He bent to cover them with his . . .

And wakened in bed, cuddling his pillow.

At 11 P.M. precisely, Henry Tait left his apartment at the back of Main Street and quickly made his way downstairs.

Emerging into the night, he swung his arms and pumped his legs vigorously, loosening up the muscles prior to his late-night run.

The double reflective strip sewn into the top of his track suit shone with a ghostly light as he jogged across Main Street. It was almost deserted now, though some of the bars and restaurants were still open. Turning down a side street, he picked up speed.

It was nearly three decades since he'd left the Marine Corps, about five years less since he came to Smallville. He'd learned a lot in the service, but nothing had stuck so fast as the words his drill sergeant bellowed.

"It's pointless me getting you fit if you don't stay fit!" the shaven-headed sergeant had roared. "You are your own responsibility!"

Henry Tait hadn't forgotten that. It was the foundation of all his beliefs. "You are your own responsibility."

He still ran twice a day, every day, barring illness. Once before dawn, before the town was awake, and again at night, when the town was closing down.

His breath came easily despite his pace. Like a lot of the guys in his platoon, he'd flirted with cigarettes and booze and marijuana. But he didn't like what they did to him, and it wasn't hard for him to adopt a lifestyle in which they played no part.

A dozen or so metal steps led up to a footbridge across the Smallville River, and Tait took them at a run. Moonlight bathed the bushes and trees in the park beyond, but he didn't stop to admire the ethereal view. He ran down the other side, coming out on the path that looped all the way around Riverside.

As he loped along, he thought he heard a noise from the bushes ahead. There it was again. A growl. Henry slowed his pace, puzzled. It didn't sound like a dog or cat. There was something . . . *alien* about the noise. It didn't belong here.

Slowing to a walk, Henry peered into the shadowed mass of bushes that dotted the rough grass, trying to make out what it could be. He saw a double flash, like eyes reflecting moonlight, and stopped short on the path.

Whatever it was, it was moving toward him.

"Hello?" he said into the mottled shadows. "Who's there?"

The growl turned into a guttural snarl. Henry had the impression of a large but sinuous body, moving quickly, crashing through the bushes as it rushed him. Instinctively, he dropped into a defensive crouch, one arm held in front of him to deflect any blow. He drew the other arm back and balled his fist.

Muggers were something you found in Metropolis, a big-city phenomenon. In Smallville, people didn't do things like this.

A dark bulk blotted out the moon, and belatedly Henry Tait realized that the figure had leaped.

He felt the weight of it as it came down on him, the impact knocking him onto his back on the grass. Hard, scaly skin rasped against him. Claws slashed at his arm, and he felt a sudden weakness there that could only be a torn muscle.

Exerting all his strength, Henry managed to get his legs doubled up underneath the snarling beast. He pushed hard, and it staggered back away him.

He rolled to his feet, his left arm hanging useless at his side. He blinked his eyes to clear them and realized blood was pouring from a gash in his forehead.

The creature sprang at him again, and he succeeded in landing a roundhouse right that drove into its ribs. But still it came on, its claws slicing deep into the flesh of his chest and belly, its fangs snapping at his throat.

He started to yell, but the claws raked painfully across his face, and his mouth filled with his own blood.

The air was full of flashing claws and ripping teeth, and Henry Tait's blood was spattered all around.

CHAPTER 5

Tuesday morning

"Morning, Victor."

Clark smiled at the driver as he gripped the handrail and swung himself up onto the school bus. Victor Kerr, the middle-aged driver, greeted him with a puzzled look.

"And you are . . . ?" he began, before breaking off in a laugh. "Hi, Clark. Glad to see you made it today. I hate to think how much it must cost your dad in gas, taking you to school every time you miss the bus."

Victor closed the door, waited till Clark seated himself, then put the engine in gear.

Clark turned to grin at Pete and Chloe, who sat together in the seat behind him. Farther back, Lana was sitting with Deanna Boyd, another of their classmates. Clark smiled at them, and to his amazement Lana's face lit up with pleasure. A smile crinkled the corners of her mouth, and her eyes twinkled.

"Infatuation alert," Pete hooted. "Clark's brain will be absent for the remainder of our trip."

Embarrassed, Clark flushed and shifted his gaze back to his friends.

"So," Chloe asked, "did you make any progress with Mr. Tait's paper?"

Clark shook his head. "It was a beautiful night. I spent it out in the barn with my telescope."

Pete winked at him. "You can see Lana's place from your den, can't you?"

"I was watching the stars, clown," Clark rejoined. Then, to Chloe: "Philosophy was the last thing on my mind."

"I watched wrestling on cable," Pete remarked. "Superficially for purposes of entertainment, but at a deeper level I was looking for existential meaning."

Chloe wrinkled her nose. "Say what?"

"There was a wrestler fighting called Johnny Plato," Pete explained. "I thought maybe I'd learn something useful from him. Like metaphysical strangleholds, maybe."

Every now and again, Clark flicked his gaze toward Lana—and each time, she appeared to be staring straight back at him, even though she was deep in conversation with Deanna. Clark didn't know whether to feel flattered or worried.

Flattered because, although he knew Lana liked him—as a friend, she always told him—romantically she was one hundred percent entwined with Whitney. Neither of them dated anyone else, and everybody expected that, when Lana turned sixteen, Whitney would present her with his ring. Making their relationship official . . . at least in the eyes of their friends.

And worried because it wasn't natural for Lana to stare at him like that.

The bus had stopped six or seven times, picking up other pupils, and it was almost a half hour before they pulled off the street and into the schoolyard.

"Whoa, what gives?" Pete asked, pointing out the window to the police patrol car parked outside the school entrance.

"Maybe they're going to frisk us for weapons," Clark suggested. "I hear they have metal detectors at the gates in Metropolis schools."

"The big city moves to Smallville," Pete replied. "Trouble in the 'hood!"

Victor cranked the door open, and they climbed down, wondering exactly who the police were looking for.

Ray Dansk shifted his body position and wakened with a jump as a droplet of water splashed off his cheek.

For a moment, lying in the darkness, he thought he was back in his cell at the pen. But there was no light streaming under his ill-fitting door, and the cacophony of two hundred men cursing and coughing and getting ready to face another miserable day was missing.

Then he remembered. He was in the cave.

Shivering, he groped in his pocket for his book of matches. His head felt heavy and thick, like he had a hangover. For some reason he couldn't figure, his heart was pounding in his chest. Something was lurking at the edge of his consciousness, as if he'd had some terrible nightmare that he couldn't quite remember. The air in the cave felt damp and muggy.

Out of habit, he reached for a cigarette, then recalled that he'd finished the pack. Strange that it didn't bother him. In jail, he felt ready to kill until he had his first daily fix of nicotine.

The match was damp and didn't catch first time against the striker. Dansk broke out in a sweat. Why was he so afraid? He struck the match again, and this time he was rewarded by a flickering yellow light. Shadows danced on the cave wall, and he saw the crumpled candy wrapper and cigarette pack from the night before, lying on the floor.

His hands felt wet and slick. From the way his T-shirt and jacket stuck to his upper body, he must have fallen asleep under a water drip. He lifted one hand closer to his face, carefully bringing up the match with the other.

The flame lit up his hands, puzzling him. They were a dull red. Screwing up his face, he examined them more closely.

Blood! His hands were covered in blood!

His pulse racing, Dansk examined his hands and wrists for a wound, but there was nothing to be seen. The match scorched his fingers and flickered out.

He pushed up his jacket sleeves, then lit another match. No scratches on his arms, either. Then what could . . . ?

Without warning, a vision swamped his senses. A half memory of crouching behind a bush, snarling like an animal. A chaos of flashing teeth and slashing claws. Blood spraying in the air around him, like a red mist.

But surely that was all a dream?

He started as a drip of water splashed down on the side of his head. Lifting the match higher, he could see where the water was soaking through from the bluff above, pooling on the cavern ceiling before falling off in a slow but steady drip.

Strange. The water wasn't colorless. It had a greenish hue, with streaks of darker green—almost emerald—twisting and roiling inside it.

Dansk shuddered and shuffled toward the exit.

The dying match picked out the exit hole's dark edges, and he froze, unable to believe what he was seeing. He stared long and hard at the thing that lay propped against the cave wall. His mouth opened in a soundless scream.

The match died and plunged him back into darkness.

His thoughts churned, trying to make sense of this. Was he still asleep, locked in the grip of a nightmare? Was he hallucinating, perhaps, some weird effect of that strange green water?

There was only one way to find out. Hands trembling, he lit another match.

The bloody, severed head still lay against the wall.

The world began to spin, and Ray Dansk fell to his knees and started to vomit.

"I regret I have a tragic announcement to make."

Principal Kwan cleared his throat, and waited for the noisy buzz of voices to subside. The entire school was crammed into the assembly hall, several hundred pupils shuffling their feet, coughing, whispering to each other, wondering what this was all about.

Standing on the dais at the front of the hall, the principal tried to find the words to break this gently. Of course, as he already knew, there were none.

"Mr. Tait, our English and philosophy teacher, was found dead this morning."

A stunned silence fell on the throng as his words sank in. He didn't give the teenagers a chance to find their voices again, but went on immediately, brusque and authoritative.

"School will continue as normal. Those pupils who feel the need for counseling, or would like someone to talk to, should report to my assistant principal, Mrs. Walker, who will make the necessary arrangements." He paused for a second. "Clark Kent and Chloe Sullivan will please remain behind and see me."

There was a sudden clamor of noise as everyone began to speak at once. The principal clapped his hands together sharply, and the sound echoed over the babble like a gunshot.

"Please," he said loudly, "go to your classes. Your teachers have been briefed and will do their best to answer your questions."

He stood and watched as they filed out of the hall, then descended from the dais to meet Clark and Chloe.

Pete Ross flicked a salted cashew in the air with his thumb. He tilted back his head, and there was a satisfying "glock" as he caught the falling nut in his open mouth.

It was lunch break, and he was sitting in the small office he, Chloe, and Clark used to produce the *Torch*. He hadn't felt like going to the lunchroom with the others from class. Quite a few of them hadn't liked Henry Tait very much; they considered him old-fashioned, a disciplinarian better suited to the military than teaching.

But Pete had always kind of liked the philosophizing ex-Marine. Where others saw him as strict, Pete thought he was fair. He didn't feel much like discussing the matter anyway. He preferred to sit here on his own and wait for his friends.

He hadn't seen Clark and Chloe since Principal Kwan asked them to stay behind. Word in the halls was they were still in the headmaster's study, being grilled by Sheriff Bryan Shugrue. Pete couldn't figure how his friends might be involved with the death of their teacher, and refused to let his imagination run away with him as he waited.

Pete was much too down-to-earth for that. You had to be when you have seven older brothers and sisters, all of whom excelled at one or more sports and academic subjects. Pete spent so much time trying to emulate them, he didn't have any left for imagination.

There was a clatter as the door opened. Pete got to his feet as Chloe and Clark entered, deep in animated conversation.

"—telling you," Chloe was saying, "this is not natural. It's tailor-made for the Wall of Weird."

"You heard Sheriff Shugrue," Clark insisted. "A wild animal. However unlikely, it's the only rational explanation."

"Private stuff?" Pete asked lightly. "Or can the invisible dude join in?"

Clark and Chloe broke off and looked at him sheepishly.

"Sorry, pal," Clark told him. "My head's so full, I didn't even see you sitting there."

Quickly, Clark and Chloe explained what had happened. Because Mr. Tait had asked them to stay after class the previous night, they'd been among the last people to see him alive.

Sheriff Shugrue had gone over their story a dozen times. Not because he suspected them of anything, but because what had happened to Henry Tait made no sense.

The teacher's body had been found that morning just after 6 A.M. Janet Cheyne worked as a cleaner at the Smallville Hotel, and her days started early. If the weather was good—and it almost always was at this time of year—Mrs. Cheyne walked to work, taking a shortcut that led through Riverside Park.

She'd thought at first that the heap she saw lying in the rough grass off the footpath was a bundle of old clothes someone had thrown away. But closer up, she saw a hand sticking out of a sleeve and bloodstains everywhere. That had been enough to send her screaming to the hotel, where the night manager called the police.

It wasn't until Bryan Shugrue's deputies were cordoning off the area, and the sheriff himself was stooping to examine the body, that he realized the head was missing.

The victim's dog-tag key-ring had his name and address engraved on the chrome. Henry Tait, 23 Appleton Tower, Smallville. He had been subjected to a frenzied attack, his flesh and clothing ripped in dozens of places by what looked like claw marks. Huge chunks of flesh had been gouged out of his shoulder and arm. The grass for yards around was stained dark with blood.

"Like he was attacked by a pack of wild dogs," Deputy Martin mused.

"More like wolves," Shugrue opined. "Or a bear, even. These are deep wounds."

"Why would a bear rip off his head—and carry it away?" Deputy Morrison asked.

Shugrue and the three deputies had spent twenty minutes looking for the head, with no success. "We're forgetting, guys," he told them, "this is Kansas. There are no wolves, or bears, or wolverines, or saber-toothed tigers."

"Tiger could be a good call, Sheriff," Martin volunteered. "As in, tiger escaped from circus. Or maybe some rich dude's private zoo."

"That's probably it," Shugrue agreed. "Martin—call the state police. Find out all you can about private zoos. Like, does Lex Luthor have one out at that place of his? And check out circuses, too, just in case."

Shugrue turned and walked away, the holstered gun, nightstick, handcuffs, and radio attached to his belt clanking as he walked. He was forty pounds overweight, and no matter how he rearranged his belt, he always clanked.

"You two stay here, secure the site. Don't allow anyone except the medics to see the body."

He strode back to the patrol car parked on the grassy riverbank. He slid into the driver's seat, and twisted the key, and his V6 Chevrolet roared into life as he spun the car's rear wheels and sent it shooting out of the park.

He'd break the news to Principal Kwan himself.

Chloe sat down at the office's computer monitor and, with a quick series of mouse clicks, logged onto the Web.

She immersed herself in the data that flashed up on-screen, as Clark finished telling their tale.

"Wolves? Bears?" Pete gasped. "In Smallville? I have to confess, Clark, I'm leaning more than a little toward Chloe's Wall of Weird proposal."

"Thank you, Peter," Chloe said, without looking around.

Hailing from the Big Met, Chloe was a relative newcomer to Smallville. It allowed her to see the place with an outsider's eye. She knew that a whole boatload of weird things had gone down in Smallville. Especially since that meteor storm hit, long before she'd even heard of the place.

She'd spent hours in the local library, poring over old news reports. Whichever way you looked at it, they could have filmed *The X-Files* here. She'd covered a whole wall of the *Torch* office with headlines and features taken from old papers and magazines. Individually, any one of them could have been found in one of the weekly supermarket tabloids.

"Local Woman Grows 50-Pound Tomato." "Student Goes Missing." "Unusual Plant Growth." "Local Puppy Born with Two Heads." "Missing Teenager Smothers Mother."

A lot of the locals blamed LuthorCorp's fertilizer plant. Who knew what chemicals and contaminants it was discharging into the atmosphere, intentionally or otherwise? Who could predict what they might do to natural cycles?

But Lionel Luthor was the town's major employer. Maybe the Wall of Weird was the price Smallville had to pay.

Chloe suspected there was another explanation, something that was connected to the meteor shower that had raked the town all those years ago. Quite what that explanation was she didn't know, but she was convinced it existed.

"Listen to this," she said now, and began reading data off

the monitor. "Phantom animal attacks. Puma-like beasts widely sighted in the British Isles, especially isolated parts of Scotland. Central and South America—hundreds of vicious attacks reported on humans and livestock. *Chupacabra,* they call it."

Clark and Pete frowned.

"It means goat-sucker," she informed them. "It savages its prey and sometimes sucks the blood. And look at that—" She gestured to a map of the western United States that had appeared on-screen. "Every one of those red dots marks a spot where what they call animal mutilations have occurred. Sometimes dozens of cattle in the one place. Suggested culprits are occult sects, secret army experiments, and phantom beasts of prey."

Pete flicked a cashew in the air. It bounced off the side of his face and fell to the floor.

"So," he asked, "what have we got in Smallville? Satanists, soldiers, or spooks?"

Clark shrugged. "It's a complete mystery to me."

"There are way too many mysteries in this town, guys." Chloe slammed her fist down on the desk. Fierce determination glinted in her eyes. "But mark my words—this one I'm going to solve!"

It was the least she could do for her favorite teacher.

All morning, Ray Dansk had sat in the corner of the cave, staring into the darkness where he'd seen that hideous object. Too scared to move, he seemed oblivious to the slow but steady trickle of water that seeped from above.

He knew the head was there, all right. He struck a match every now and then, as if hoping that this time it would have disappeared.

But the book of matches was almost done. He only had a few left.

Worse—he was sure he recognized the bloody face. That pencil-thin mustache . . . those eyes that had once held him in contempt. It was Henry Tait.

Dansk's thoughts swooped and raced in circles. He'd had a dream. He'd dreamed that Henry Tait had died in an orgy of bloody savagery. Now Henry Tait's head was here, mere feet away from him.

Dansk shuddered. He could feel those dead eyes boring into him, accusing. "It wasn't me," he wanted to shout. "I didn't do anything."

By late afternoon, hunger pangs were gnawing at his belly. He took the candy bars from his pocket, sodden and crushed. The thought of trying to eat one filled him with nausea.

He sat with his back pressed hard against the dank wall, hugging his knees to his chest and wishing he was back in his warm cell in the Metropolis Penitentiary.

CHAPTER 6

Tuesday night

The white kid driving gloves fit snug as a second skin.

Lex Luthor's hand closed around the black leather gearshift and flicked it smoothly into first. He revved the gas pedal and dropped the clutch simultaneously, and the silver Porsche bulleted across the spotlit parking lot outside the fertilizer plant.

The day shift had gone home, the night crew had started, and Lex couldn't think of a single excuse for staying in his office a minute longer. Although paperwork bored him, he applied himself to it with the same indefatigable efficiency and charm that defined his whole life. Now, for the first time in weeks, his in-tray was empty.

He celebrated by going from zero to sixty in seconds, and the sleek sports car shot out through the factory gate.

Lex had been in Smallville for almost a year, and he still had no idea why he was here. His father Lionel claimed it was to give him hands-on experience running a business, with the opportunity to turn a money-losing operation into a profitable one. "Business is war," Lionel had impressed on his son since he was a child. "To survive, you have to win your battles."

But Lex always suspected there was more to it. He was a suspicious man in many ways.

And, more often than not, his suspicions proved to be well-founded.

In the blaze of his headlamps he could see the road fork

ahead. Deftly, Lex steered the car down the right lane. Within seconds, he was racing along a single-track road. On either side of him, row upon row of head-high cornstalks marched off into the moonlit distance.

Lex gave an involuntary shudder. He'd been here the day of the meteor strike, a nine-year-old kid dragged along by his father to witness some deal where the old man would cheat with promises that he'd never keep and that lawyers could never crack.

Bored by the adults' talk, Lex had taken advantage of the hot afternoon to wander off into the corn rows. The boy felt strangely alive. No father nagging him. No asthma attack that necessitated the hated inhaler he had to carry everywhere with him. No pressure on him to pass exams, to get everything right, to be his father's son and succeed, succeed, succeed. Just a little boy with a thick thatch of orange hair, glorying in the summer sun, lulled by the buzzing of the cornbugs.

And then hell came to Earth.

He'd looked up from the cracked and dusty soil to see something streaking through the sky, trailing a plume of dirty smoke. It was heading directly for him.

Lex turned on his heels and ran for all he was worth. Within twenty yards he was gasping and wheezing, as his lungs refused to function properly. Still trying to run, he fumbled the inhaler from his pocket. But before he could raise it to his lips, and suck in the sweet, clear oxygen, he tripped and fell headlong.

The inhaler went flying from his hand. Lex scrabbled desperately to retrieve it, even as the air filled with the stench of sulfur and burning rock, and the blue skies above his head were blotted out with dark, menacing smoke.

He remembered hearing an explosion, then everything faded to black.

Lex still didn't know exactly what had happened that day. His father called in the most expensive doctors his money could buy. Lex was flown to Havana on the LuthorCorp private jet. But the Cuban specialists, widely recognized to be the best in the world, were as baffled as their U.S. counterparts.

Whatever had happened, Lex underwent a miracle cure. He never suffered from asthma again.

And if the price he had to pay for that was losing every hair on his head, with a medical guarantee it would never grow back, then so be it.

But it was a mystery. And Lex Luthor didn't like mysteries until they were solved. With a certainty that bordered on arrogance, he knew that one day he would solve this one, too.

Meantime, Renata Meissen was the mystery he was currently working on. She'd come on to him as if their affair had never ended, and Lex had played along. No harm in enjoying a puzzle while you tried to solve it.

Lex smiled softly to himself as the car, almost an extension of his own body, cleaved through the night like a silver dagger.

"I just can't get over it," Martha Kent said, for perhaps the tenth time since Clark had returned from school. "Henry Tait was such a gentleman. This town will miss him."

They'd eaten their evening meal in silence, the three of them lost in their own thoughts. Martha remembered Henry as the man who'd awakened her own interest in philosophy during one of the night study courses she'd attended.

Clark, too, had only known him as a teacher. Mr. Tait had been hard on him, but always fair. Clark never felt the teacher singled him out and always had the impression the man only wanted to help. He obviously burned with such a love of philosophy himself, he couldn't understand why every single of one his students didn't feel it, too.

Jonathan Kent was trying hard not to prejudge a man. He hadn't known Henry Tait all that well. They'd shared a beer a couple of times, on the rare occasions Jonathan went into town at night. They'd chatted at PTA meetings and school parties. Jonathan probably wouldn't even have remembered that Henry had been a witness for the prosecution in the Dansk case . . .

If he hadn't seen Ray Dansk himself, that very afternoon.

It has to be a coincidence, he told himself. According to Clark, Tait was mauled to death by some wild animal—that was the official line the police were taking. The way he looked out in the fields yesterday afternoon, Ray Dansk would have been hard-pressed to maul a puppy.

And Dansk had been open about the fact he was looking for work, looking to go straight. Why would he even have allowed himself to be seen, if he was really after revenge on Henry Tait? It just didn't make sense.

If Jonathan called Bryan Shugrue with his vague suspicions, and the sheriff hauled Dansk in for questioning, it might destroy any chance the man ever stood of building himself a decent life.

Jonathan started as he heard the sound of a car horn blaring outside.

"It's for me." Clark excused himself and went to wash his hands at the sink. "Lex called earlier," he said, almost guiltily. "He's going to give me a ride into town."

Jonathan frowned. He'd seen the trouble Lionel Luthor brought to Smallville, lying and cheating when there had been no real need. He had no proof that Lex was the same, driven by an ambition that could never be slaked. Jonathan had long since learned that it didn't pay to take chances, at least not where people were concerned. It was too soon to gauge how far Lex had fallen from his father's tree.

He opened his mouth to protest, but Martha quickly hushed him. "Have fun, Clark," she called to their son, as he hurried out the kitchen door. "And don't be back too late."

Jonathan sighed and shook his head as Martha smiled at him. "He's a teenager, Jonathan," she reminded him. "Life's an adventure. Let him live it."

"He's no normal teenager," Jonathan pointed out. "I just worry about him giving himself away. You know, someone finding out about his powers. Lex Luthor is the kind of sharp operator who might just do that."

"Clark knows to be careful."

Reluctantly, Jonathan nodded his agreement. They'd had this conversation a thousand times over the years. How to strike a balance between concealing the fact that Clark was far from being an ordinary child and trying to allow him to grow up like one. Because if anyone found out the truth, Jonathan would stake the farm that it would be the end of a normal life for Clark.

The boy would become a bug in some government lab. He'd be tested and probed and measured, as they looked for ways to unleash his powers for political or military ends. Or he might even be caged, held prisoner by an uncomprehending, frightened world, which would know only that a teenage boy had the power to lift cars, see through solid walls, and run at sixty miles an hour.

At the end of the day, they could do no more than trust Clark himself.

And if—as Jonathan liked to think—they'd brought him up to share the values he and Martha held at the core of their own lives, then Clark wouldn't let any of them down.

If he did, Jonathan would have only himself to blame.

Huddled alone in his stifling, dank cave, Ray Dansk had lost all track of time. With no light and shade for guidance, he couldn't tell if it was day or night. He tried counting off the seconds, but lost count so many times that in the end he gave up.

Completely deprived of any form of stimulation, his mind started to play tricks on him.

He'd read a magazine story in prison, an examination of sensory deprivation and its use in personal development. According to the author, "floating" in an isolation tank cleared the mind, stimulated the body's autoimmune system, and had so many benefits it was being touted as a miracle.

But what Dansk remembered was the description of the downside of isolation. Scientists had experimented with a group of U.S. Marines, the toughest men they could find. A high percentage of them emerged from the isolation tanks after only a few minutes of darkness, screaming in terror or crying like babies.

Now Dansk understood why. Every now and again Henry Tait's severed head seemed to shine with an eldritch inner glow that lit up even the cave's darkest recesses. Hardly able to tell what was real and what was hallucination, Dansk descended deeper into his own personal hell.

Worst of all was when the head spoke to him.

"Why?" it asked him, the voice grating and accusing. "Why did you kill me?"

Dansk trembled in terror at the silence that followed. With shaking hand he coaxed a precious match into life, hoping to set his mind at rest. In the flickering light, he could see the head still propped against the entrance wall. Dansk caught his breath. Was it closer? Had it moved toward him?

The match flared suddenly, burning his fingers. Cursing, he dropped it. It landed in a pool of water, and sputtered out. Dansk made to tear off another match—there were only two left now—but the matchbook fell from his shaking hands.

Frantically, he crawled forward on his hands and knees, reaching out in the darkness, fumbling for his only source of light.

Got it! He lifted the soggy cardboard, and it disintegrated in his hand. *Useless!*

No more light.

The realization terrified him. At any moment he expected to hear the voices of the Smallville deputies, smashing down the entrance barrier, barging into his bolthole with guns drawn. But surely it wouldn't be prison this time. There were worse places. Much worse.

"I'm not insane," he repeated over and over to himself, as if the mantra itself would be enough to guarantee him sanity.

But what sane man killed for no reason and decapitated his victim as an afterthought? No judge or jury would believe him. He'd be condemned to a mental institution, forced to live the rest of his life as a madman tormented by visions of his evil deeds.

Tears filled his eyes and spilled down his face. When he put up a hand to brush them away, his skin felt rough and scaly. His chest was itching again, as if the dragon tattoo that covered it was writhing under his skin. As if . . .

As if it were alive.

I'm infected! The thought came to him with startling clarity, out of nowhere. *I've caught some sort of disease. I'm going to die!*

◆◆◆

Gee forces crushed Clark against the interior of the door as Lex swung the car through a right-angled bend at fifty miles an hour.

Lex flicked the gearshift from third into fourth as they exited from the tight curve. The sports car's ultralow-profile tires bit into the road, and they catapulted into the night with Jimi Hendrix's "Voodoo Chile" blaring from the eight-speaker sound system.

"Some car," Clark said admiringly.

Lex gave a slight smile. "When you pay for the best, you expect the best," he agreed. "But at the end of the day, Clark, a car is all it is. A means of getting from point A to point B."

"A lot more entertainingly than my dad's pickup!"

Lex's smile broadened. Despite the six-year age gap between them, Lex really liked the teenager. The kid was straight as an arrow. He possessed a solid set of values, which some might call old-fashioned but which Lex appreciated for what they were. Morals in an immoral world.

And Clark wasn't afraid to stand up for what he believed in. In the gray world of yes-men and flunkies that made up much of Lex's life, Clark stood out like a beacon. He was almost the kid brother that Lex had never had.

And plus, of course, Clark had saved Lex's life.

It happened on Lex's very first day back in Smallville. He hadn't been in the best of moods, angry that his father had exiled him to this unbelievably isolated backwater of a town, to manage the most boring plant in the LuthorCorp empire. But Lex had learned the hard way not to allow his emotions to determine his behavior—a result, perhaps, of having a cold and distant superachiever for a father.

He'd been driving toward town the way he always drove—fast, precise and efficient. But even the best of drivers can be caught out by the unexpected. As he approached the Old Mill Bridge, his front tires ran over a bale of barbed wire that had fallen from an overloaded farm truck. The tires exploded into shreds, and the car swerved violently toward the bridge.

Lex fought in vain to regain control, sparks shrieking from the bare wheel rims as they gouged the road.

There's a kid on the bridge! I'm going to hit him!

Desperately, Lex wrenched the steering wheel to full lock. But it was too late. The car broadsided. As if in slow motion, Lex saw the startled look on the kid's face as a ton and a half of high-tech sports car skidded toward him.

There was a loud bang as the vehicle smashed through the bridge's retaining wall. Then everything was tumbling over and over.

Did I hit the kid? Flash of blue sky. Flash of flowing water.

Lex's head snapped forward, slamming into the dashboard as the car arced down through the air and hit the river.

Next thing Lex knew, he was coming to at the side of the road. The teenager was bending over him, soaking wet, hands on Lex's chest as he tried to pump the water from his lungs.

The kid's name was Clark Kent. He said the car had narrowly missed him as it broke through the bridge wall. When Lex didn't surface, Clark had dived in, managed to free the unconscious man from the wreckage, and swum with him to safety.

It wasn't until later, when Lex had the car salvaged from its watery grave, that he realized there was a mystery here. The car's roof had been peeled back like an old-fashioned sardine can.

When Lex asked Clark about it, the teenager just shrugged. "Must have been the way it scraped along the river bottom," he suggested.

Lex accepted the explanation, but didn't really buy it. Now and again, he found himself wondering if Clark himself had somehow ripped open the car roof. But how could any-one—let alone a fifteen-year-old—do something like that?

And that was another reason Lex liked Clark. The kid was a challenge.

A mystery for Lex to solve.

Lex's silence didn't faze Clark. They knew each other well enough to feel relaxed in the other's company.

"You know a friend by what they don't say," his mother had told him once. Since meeting Lex, he'd learned what her words meant.

Clark leaned back against the headrest and allowed the music to wash over him.

That was another thing about Lex. One day he'd be listening to late-sixties psychedelia, the next it would be speed metal from twenty years later, and the day after that it would be reggae or hip-hop. His tastes were eclectic, and impeccable.

Clark banished all thought from his mind, letting the music lift him as he watched the headlights carving a path through the night.

Whitney Fordman swung his gleaming four-by-four into the parking space, yanked on the emergency brake, and switched off the engine. He slid out of the cab and stepped down onto the tarmac, turning back to admire the car as he walked away. He almost felt like giving it a friendly pat, as if it were a pet rather than a vehicle.

It was the best truck in town, a gift from his father to celebrate Whitney's being named captain of the Smallville Crows football team. Gulping a deep breath of the cool night air, Whitney drew back his shoulders and sauntered over to the Beanery.

Lana should be waiting for him there.

Sometimes, Whitney couldn't believe his luck. The coolest cab around. Big-money sponsorship for his intended pro football career. And Lana Lang, the prettiest girl this side of Metropolis.

The Golden Couple, some of the other lettermen called them. Whitney liked that. It felt real good to be the dude who had it all.

He pushed open the Beanery's glass door, and was immediately assailed by the odor of roasting coffee. This was where all his friends hung out—and every other kid from school. In Smallville, there was no place else to go.

He waved a general greeting to the dozen or so teenagers who sat around the booths and tables, casting his eyes around for Lana. He felt a stab of disappointment. She wasn't there. He glanced at his watch. Not like her to keep him waiting. His disappointment turned into a slight irritation.

He called to Vikki, the waitress, for a cup of regular coffee, and lowered himself into a chair at a table where three of his football buddies sat. There was some discussion of what might have happened to Henry Tait, but within minutes they were deep in an animated replay of several of last season's most successful games.

"—remember that quarterback? The guy from Flemyngton?" Whitney was saying a short while later, when one of his teammates nodded to him.

"That's Lana coming in."

"She'll wait," Whitney said confidently. "Let me finish my story first."

He was sitting with his back to the restaurant's entrance, but he could see Lana's reflection in the mirror behind the counter. In her T-shirt and tight jeans, she looked beautiful as she stood just inside the doorway, acknowledging the others' greetings.

Then he saw the door open behind her, and Clark Kent and Lex Luthor entered together.

Whitney broke off his tale in midsentence and got to his feet. He didn't much like Kent. He was a couple of years younger than Whitney, but he was in Lana's class, and Whitney figured he was infatuated with her. Lana had promised him they were only good friends, neighbors who'd lived within a mile of each other for a decade. But Whitney was jealous, anyway.

The less time she spent with Kent, the happier Whitney felt.

"Hi, Lana," he heard Kent say, as he walked over slowly to join his girlfriend.

A broad smile played on Whitney's lips as he came up behind Lana and gently took her arm. "Hi, babe. How come you're late?"

He was astounded by her reply.

"Oh, you know—things to do." Lana shrugged casually, as if it was of no importance. Then she turned away from him, cutting him dead.

"Mind if I sit with you, Clark?" she asked.

Whitney's mouth literally fell open in amazement as he watched the flustered Kent nod in surprise, then lead Lana to a table.

As they sat down together, Lex Luthor remained standing. "Three's a crowd, guys," he said hastily. "Besides, I have stuff to do."

Lex leaned down, bending his face close to Clark's ear. "Nice going, Clark," he said in a stage whisper, just loud enough for Whitney to hear. "You make a great couple."

Bald-headed freak! Whitney glowered as Lex headed for the door, calling back to Kent over his shoulder.

"See you tomorrow night, Clark. We have some serious planning to do."

The restaurant door swung closed behind him, and still Whitney stood openmouthed in the center of the floor. A couple of girls at a nearby table giggled, and he suddenly flushed with embarrassment as it came home to him what had just happened.

Lana Lang—his girlfriend—had dumped him.

"Lana, I don't want to sound impertinent," Clark began diffidently, "but did you *mean* to do what you just did?"

Lana tossed her long, dark hair and stared at him, as if not grasping what he was alluding to. "You mean Whitney?" she said at last. "I didn't really do anything." She leaned across the table until her face was only six inches away from his.

Clark braced himself. The necklace Lana often wore made him feel atrocious anytime he was within a few feet of her. But tonight, he was relieved to see that the green-jeweled pendant wasn't around Lana's neck.

"Anyway," she went on, her blue eyes fixed on his, "I don't want to talk about Whitney. Let's find a more interesting subject."

Clark was incredulous. He'd worshiped Lana from afar for years, and yet she had never shown the slightest interest in him. At least, not romantic interest. They were good friends, true, but their friendship had never progressed beyond that.

"Neighbors—classmates—but I don't know a lot about you, Clark. Any hobbies?"

"Um, astronomy. But I guess you'd find that boring."

"Let me be the judge." Lana's smile seemed to light up the whole room. "Tell me all about it."

Clark felt faint. He had hoped—dreamed—prayed that one day she might notice him.

He was almost afraid to admit that it looked like his dream was coming true.

Neither of them even noticed as Whitney, his face red

with angry embarrassment, stalked out of the restaurant and stormed off into the night.

Ray Dansk no longer knew if he was awake or asleep.

The itch in his chest had become intolerable. His fingernails seemed to be elongating, becoming blade-sharp claws. He probed his teeth with his tongue. It felt like there were hundreds of them.

Ridiculous! I have to get out of here. I'll wait till morning, and make my move.

But as far as he knew, it could be morning now. He had no way of knowing. How long had he been here, anyway? Hours? Or was it days?

He shuddered, and his whole body began to shake. He started toward where he thought the exit was, then remembered its grim guardian. Henry Tait's severed head.

He was more a prisoner now than he'd ever been in jail.

It's not fair. I don't deserve this!

Sudden anger flared through him. The shivering stopped at once, as if his rage was enough to warm him. *No, I don't deserve this. I've paid my debt. The score is settled. I'm due a new start. It's my right, damn it. My right!*

A red mist swam in front of his eyes, interspersed with flecks of shining green. He felt the dragon coiling across his chest, ruffling its scales, its fiery breath searing him. A low snarl escaped from his lips, and he started with surprise. He sounded more like a wild beast than a human being.

Why should I be trapped here? Why should I suffer more and more? I'm Ray Dansk, damn it. I'm a Smallville Dragon!

♦♦♦

"It's so beautiful at night."

The silvery moon was high in the sky, its pale light falling on the endless rows of corn, as the night breeze rippled their stalks and made them sway.

"They're like the ocean," Lana said quietly. "Like waves on the ocean."

Clark walked beside her up the dirt road leading home. Their hands were clasped together, completely lost in each other's company.

They'd talked for hours, oblivious to everyone else in the restaurant, unaware that they were being watched and whispered about. Fast on their way to becoming tomorrow's school gossip.

They'd talked about everything, and nothing. And when they were silent, their eyes did their talking for them.

It's like we've known each other all our lives, Clark thought. And, of course, they had.

Lana's hand was warm in his, and he found himself wishing the long walk home could last forever. Tonight had been . . . perfect.

All too soon they saw the lights in the windows of Nell Potter's country house. They stopped a hundred yards away, as if by mutual consent, though neither spoke a word. Clark took Lana's other hand in his and drew her gently around to face him.

"Please don't take this the wrong way," he began hesitantly. "But this is all so . . . so unexpected." She reached a finger to his lips to hush him, but Clark knew that for his own peace of mind he had to go on. "Whitney's always been your boyfriend. Has something happened to change your feelings? Am I . . . ?"

His voice tailed away, afraid to vocalize what he feared.

"Are you just a way of making Whitney jealous?" Lana finished for him. "No. You're not. You're a good-looking boy with a great personality." She smiled at him, and Clark's heart leaped. "I want to get to know you better. Much better."

She turned away briefly, looking toward her aunt's house. "Twelve years I've lived with Aunt Nell. We've been neighbors all that time, and friends for most of it. Yet we've never even kissed."

She leaned closer against him, and automatically Clark's arms moved around her waist. He could smell her delicate perfume, feel the warmth of her body through her clothes.

"Thank you for tonight," she went on. "I don't think I've been so happy since . . . before my parents died."

Her eyelids fluttered closed, and her head tilted back.

Clark looked down at her, almost pained by her beauty. There was nothing in the world he wanted more than to kiss her, to hold her tight and tell her he loved her, he'd always loved her, he always would love her.

And yet—how could he? The meteor strike that killed Lewis and Laura Lang had also brought the spacecraft carrying Clark Kent to Earth. In some terrible way, he felt personally responsible for their deaths. It was his fault that Lana was an orphan. He blamed himself for many of the strange things that had happened in Smallville since that awful day.

Guilt ripped through him, so painful it was almost physical. How could he kiss the girl he loved when it had been his arrival that destroyed her life?

He stifled a sigh, then bent to plant a gentle, lingering kiss on Lana's forehead.

Her eyes opened in surprise, but he affected not to notice. "Mom told me not to be late," he said lamely. "I'll see you at school tomorrow."

Then Lana was alone, staring after him in surprise and disappointment as he disappeared into the rows of corn, as if he'd been swallowed up by the ocean.

CHAPTER 7

Wednesday

"What's the problem, Romeo?" Chloe greeted Clark as he entered the *Torch* office at lunchtime. "Juliet having second thoughts?"

"Excuse me?"

"Why are you gracing me with your presence, when you could be enjoying a cozy tête-à-tête with Lana?" Chloe gave a mock-shiver. "Man, you should have seen the two of you on the bus this morning, holding hands and giggling like a couple of ten-year-olds."

She considered for a moment. "Actually, I'm not sure ten-year-olds behave like that. Amend to six-year-olds!"

School had been abnormally subdued since the previous day's tragic discovery. But gossip about Lana's public dumping of Whitney and her sudden interest in Clark had spread like wildfire. *Strange,* Chloe thought, *that a trivial piece of personal business should provoke more discussion than the death of a respected teacher.*

Not that Henry Tait's death had been so quickly forgotten. The official police conclusion—tentative though it was—held that Tait had been mauled and mutilated by an unknown animal. His body had been shipped to Metropolis for forensic examination, but Bryan Shugrue had made it known he didn't expect the big-city experts to cast any new light on the strange death.

"Lana's doing some extra studying in the library," Clark

explained. "I thought you might appreciate a hand with the next issue."

Chloe made no move to return to the computer on the desk before her. She hesitated, wondering if she was about to make a mistake. But no, she and Clark had become good friends since her first, lonely days in Smallville. In similar circumstances, she'd expect him to be straight with her.

"Don't you find it suspicious?" she asked. "I mean, Lana has been going out with Whitney since the Bronze Age. They're an item. Why would she just dump the guy and switch her affections to you? No offense, Clark, but Whitney sure holds all the aces in the status stakes."

"A woman's fickle mind?" Clark suggested, in a weak attempt at a joke. Then he shrugged. "I don't know what made Lana change her mind. All I know is, I'm glad she did."

He lowered himself into a seat and swiveled it to face her. "Now—what are we working on?"

But Chloe wasn't to be fobbed off as easily as that. "Like, the sudden switch might be viewed as borderline weird," she persisted. "Could be Lana's turnabout is somehow connected to all the other weird goings-on in Smallville. Don't you think?"

"I'm trying not to think," Clark snapped back. "It's time I gave my brain a vacation and let myself have a little fun."

Pity you couldn't have it with me, Chloe thought wistfully. Behind her tough facade, she really liked Clark. She wouldn't have minded being in Lana's place.

"Now—what are we working on?" Clark asked again, and she knew that the subject was closed.

"The death of Mr. Tait," she told him, gesturing toward the screen, on which the dead teacher's photograph and details were displayed. "No point us trying to cover it from a news point of view, though—the local press have already got the story."

She glanced at Clark and felt irritated when she saw his gaze wasn't on the screen. "I thought I'd write an obituary," she tried again, "only expanded, like the story of his life. I accessed the record files at the public library and came up with something interesting. Twelve years ago, Henry Tait was a witness in a court case. The perp was convicted partly on the basis of his evidence."

She paused, glaring fiercely at her friend. "Clark, are you even listening?"

"Mmm," Clark responded, making it even more obvious that he wasn't.

Chloe shook her head in exasperation. "Beat it, Kent," she told him, turning back to her monitor. "You're no use to man or beast like this."

She saw from the look on his face that he didn't have a clue what she was talking about.

"Oh," she exploded, "go take a cold shower!"

Clark felt like he was hovering two inches above the ground as he walked along the corridor to the cafeteria. He'd hardly slept last night. What need did he have of dreams when it looked like his dreams were coming true? His whole body was effused with a warm glow that strengthened every time he thought of Lana.

Cliché or not, he thought, *we're made for each other.*

Someone stepped out from behind a pillar, barring his way.

Whitney. He looked as if he hadn't slept, either. His eyes were red and bleary, and he sported a slight stubble from not having shaved.

"I want to know what's going on, Kent. What's with you and Lana?"

"Whitney, I'm sorry, but—"

Clark broke off as Whitney took a step closer, thrusting his face forward aggressively. His voice was harsh and grating. "That's not what I asked you, farm boy," he snarled. "Is this some kind of scam Lana's pulling, to make me jealous or something?"

Clark shook his head. "Look, Whitney," he went on, trying to sound reasonable, "you don't own Lana. She makes her own choices."

"She already chose, wiseass. She chose me. We're going to Luthor's party together on Saturday."

"Well, I think Lana has changed her mind."

"Don't patronize me!" Whitney's hand came up, and he jabbed a finger into Clark's chest. "Why would she choose a geek like you over me?"

Clark stared coolly at the older boy, restraining his anger. One of the first lessons Mom and Dad had taught him was that he always had to be in control of himself. With strength like his, he couldn't afford to get involved in a fight. Not ever.

"Please, Whitney," he said appeasingly, "I think we should just let it drop."

His words were meant to calm the situation, but they had the opposite effect. Whitney's eyes flashed with anger, and he clenched his fist as he drew back his hand.

In slow motion, Clark saw the fist shoot directly at his face. He couldn't afford to let the blow land. Not for his own sake, because his body was much tougher and hardier than the average human's.

He had to avoid the blow for Whitney's sake, because if it landed, the quarterback was likely to break his fist.

Faster than the eye could follow, Clark jerked his head to one side.

Whitney's fist whistled past his jaw. Before the surprised football star could stop its momentum, his hand slammed hard into the hall wall.

As Whitney yelped with pain, Clark stepped around him
to resume his journey.

"You haven't heard the last of this, Kent," Whitney raged
at his retreating back. "Believe me, you'll be sorry!"

Sure, Clark thought. *Surprising what a farm boy can do.*

Sunset painted the sky with purple and gold.

Trapped in the shifting shadows of his own mind, Ray
Dansk's world was a thousand shades of red. Red for anger
and fury. Red for rage.

Red for revenge.

He'd started out with good intentions. He'd sworn never
to break the law again. He'd even been willing to take a job,
working on some pig-stinking farm.

And what's his payback? Cooped up in a hole, starving
and soaking and shaking and sweating. Even the punishment
cells in jail were better than this. At least you were fed, got
to shower and take some exercise.

As his thoughts spiraled in dark, turbulent circles, Dansk
flexed his muscles continuously. Readying himself for attack out of the darkness? He could no longer tell if he was
just thinking, or if the words were really spewing from his
mouth.

He'd heard voices earlier, faint and far away. At first he'd
thought it was the disembodied head, come to haunt him
again. But the head had spoken clearly and firmly. These
voices were muffled and barely audible.

Kids come to play, he thought, in a rare moment of lucid-
ity.

But no, these voices were too deep, too mature, to be
kids. Besides, kids didn't call each other "Chief." It had to
be the cops, come to check out the caves in their search for

Tait's murderer. Come for him. Come to shackle him, and beat him, and lock him away.

He sat there for what seemed like hours, not making a sound, doing his best not to even breathe. Until finally he could hear the voices no more.

Anger welled up in him again, then, erupting like lava from a long-pent-up volcano, boiling through his brain like acid.

This wasn't his fault. Why was *he* suffering, when the real villains were escaping scot-free?

He knew who to blame. Three of them, three nosy creeps who couldn't stop themselves interfering in other people's business. He knew who they were.

"Justice," they'd called it when they locked him away. Well, now one of them was dead. That was justice, too. The others would soon follow.

Ray Dansk flexed his claws and raked them slowly down the cave wall. He was getting out of here. It was time for the Dragon to roar.

"You know, Clark, this farm would have ground me into the dust long ago if you hadn't come along."

Jonathan was lying on his back on the floor of the barn, using a flashlight to search for the fuel leak on his pickup truck. Clark had grasped the vehicle's front fender and lifted it off the ground without so much as breaking sweat. Now, as he effortlessly held the heavy truck, his father grunted with satisfaction.

"I see it. Loose screw on the feed pipe connection. Hold it just a second—" There was a pause as he twisted the screwdriver. "Okay, all done."

He pushed himself out from under the truck and got to his

feet. Even after all these years, after all the examples he'd
seen of his son's amazing strength, he never failed to be impressed by what Clark could do.

The boy lowered the truck gently to the floor.

"Yes, sir," Jonathan said again. "If it hadn't been for you,
I'd have gone the way of Rudy Malone and Ernie Deever,
and every other farmer who's given up and quit the land."

"I'm just glad I can be of help, Dad," Clark said modestly. Hesitating, he stared hard at his father, then rushed on.
"Dad, how can you tell if you're in love?"

Jonathan sighed. Sometimes he had to force himself to
remember that Clark was no longer a boy, but a young man.
This past year in particular, he'd really seemed to mature.

Still, Jonathan was glad his son could talk to him about
such things. A lot of kids and their parents drifted apart precisely because they didn't talk to each other. He and Martha
had always tried to be open and honest with their boy, to
trust him, and in return allow him to learn to trust them.

They tried to be his friends, as well as his parents.

"We-ell," Jonathan replied slowly, "you just sort of
know . . . I guess." He figured Clark was referring to Lana,
but it would have been insensitive to come out and say it.
"When you want to be with someone all the time. When
you're just as happy shopping as you would have been playing ball."

He saw Clark nod and smile, and Jonathan felt happy for
him. He himself had discovered all about love the day he
met Martha. Their life together ever since had been a joyful
learning experience. Although it could easily have turned
out otherwise . . .

Jonathan was dating Nell Potter at the time. But when
Martha came into his life, she unleashed a whirlwind in his
heart. He found himself having to make the kind of decision

any man would envy. To turn his back on one beautiful girl, because he'd fallen in love with another.

Clark was heading for the barn door, off to wash up before dinner. The deep purple cast by the fading sun wreathed the farmyard beyond.

"Wait up," Jonathan called after him. "There's more."

Clark stopped and turned back, his face expectant.

"Real love isn't the be-all and end-all," Jonathan cautioned. "I'm not so old that I don't remember how it feels. You flush when she enters the room. Your heart races, just thinking about her. But that's not the target, Clark. It's just the starting point. Real love . . ." His voice trailed away as he sought the right words.

"Real love is the foundation on which you build the rest of your life."

◆◆◆

The nearest streetlight was a hundred yards away, yet its orange sodium glow stabbed at Dansk's eyes like daggers. He blinked slowly, several times. After so long in the oppressive darkness of the cave, his optic nerves needed time to adjust.

Driven by the anger that coursed through his nervous system, he had come to a sudden decision. Screwing his resolve to the maximum, he'd slithered across the cave floor toward the exit hole. He couldn't see the severed head, but he could feel its malevolent presence as he tried to skirt around it.

Groping for the yawning cleft with one hand, his fingers brushed against Henry Tait's blood-matted hair. He howled in terror, lashing out with his hand. There was a thud as his blow connected, and he heard the head roll aside on the uneven floor.

Ha! So much for you, Henry Bigmouth Tait!

Galvanized by his own courage, he lowered himself carefully down into the main chamber.

Free! The word reverberated in his mind as he half ran, half skidded across the cave floor. It had been so long since he'd used his leg muscles, it was hard to make them obey him.

Reaching the barrier boards, he peered out through a chink in the wood. His eyes strained finally to *see* something after his long hours of blind solitude.

He breathed a sigh of relief. It was night.

He could tell from a bright silver glow that the moon was rising someplace out of view, and a few early stars twinkled above. Satisfied there was nobody around, he squeezed under the boards and rolled clumsily to his feet.

He scrambled into the comforting shadows cast by a clump of bushes and waited for his eyes to stop hurting.

It was almost ten minutes before he moved again. Keeping low to the ground, he darted into the shade of a thick tree trunk. From there, he made his way slowly along the riverbank, hugging the shadows.

There was a phone booth in the center of the park, he remembered. That's where he'd find what he needed.

Five minutes later he was squinting his eyes against the booth light, swinging open the door and snatching the directory chained to the shelf.

He thumbed quickly through the pages. The words seemed to make no sense to him, as if he'd forgotten how to read. But he concentrated hard, and at last the names and addresses swam mistily into focus.

He stopped at a page and ran his finger down the list of surnames. Not here. Impatiently he ripped the page from the book and tossed it aside. There . . . on the next page was the entry he sought.

Verne, Louis   Smallville 45054, followed by his address—which Dansk recognized as being the address of the Luthor mansion.

The creep must have come up in the world.

Ray Dansk threw the book from him with an ugly snarl of triumph.

CHAPTER 8

Wednesday night

Gravel crunched under Clark's feet as he walked up the long, sweeping driveway that led to the Luthor mansion.

He could see the ancient Scottish castle up ahead, beyond the fringe of trees that surrounded it. Silhouetted against the rising moon, it seemed to exude an aura of grim foreboding, if not downright menace. For the first time in weeks, thick clouds scudded across the sky.

History wasn't Clark's strongest subject, but Lex had told him the castle's story. Originally built nearly eight hundred years earlier, in the thirteenth century, its first owners were the chieftains of a Scottish clan. Over the centuries, the castle had seen more than its share of warfare and death.

When the armies of the English king, Edward I, invaded Scotland, the castle was burned and its defenders massacred. Edward commanded it to be rebuilt, with strengthened defenses and a massive new great hall. When he died, the Scots revolted against his heir. The English armies went home and left the castle to its fate.

Kings and clan chiefs had come and gone, but the castle endured beyond them all.

It had been a near ruin when Lionel Luthor first saw it. At massive expense, he'd had it dismantled stone by stone and shipped it to Smallville, where one of America's finest architects oversaw its complete reconstruction.

Now, as he drew closer to the forbidding stone walls, Clark could imagine muskets protruding from the narrow

slit windows. Wild, kilted soldiers had fought to the death
on these battlements, and the spiral stone stairways had wit-
nessed a hundred bloody sword fights.

What was that?

Clark's mind had drifted off ancient history, and his
thoughts turned to Lana, when he thought he heard a noise
in the layer of rhododendron bushes that sprouted beneath
the stately beech trees lining the drive. There was a loud
rustling, followed by a low growl.

Clark stood for a moment, senses keen, listening intently.
Nothing, save the light wind soughing through the branches.
He focused his eyes and trained them on the bushes, striving
to penetrate the shadows with his peculiar vision. Nothing.

Shrugging, he moved on.

Fifteen feet above ground level, crouched in a fork in the
branches of a beech tree, Ray Dansk's eyes glittered cruelly.

He watched in silence as the figure of a teenage boy resumed his journey toward the gatehouse, where the castle
entry stood. He saw the boy push a button on the gatehouse
wall. There was a flash of light as the door opened, then the
boy disappeared inside.

Dansk ran his tongue over his teeth. Strange, how much
sharper they seemed to be. And his skin . . . it felt so hard,
and scaly. Under his leathers and T-shirt, the dragon tattoo
was pulsing in time to his heartbeat.

He'd been infected, all right. By what, he had no idea—
for sometimes his thoughts and emotions didn't seem to be
his at all. They seemed . . . alien. Hey, but who was com-
plaining? He hadn't had a cigarette in . . . he didn't know
how long. But it was a while. He'd been a thirty-a-day

smoker since his midteens, yet the craving for nicotine had melted away like ice in the sun.

Maybe he'd been infected by something good.

Red fire burned in his heart as he dropped from the branch he clung to and slithered down the wide main trunk.

More like a reptile than a human.

"Lex is waiting for you in the armory lounge," Louis Verne announced to Clark.

They stood just inside the gatehouse, which had been restored to all its former glory. Several suits of armor from different periods stood guard at the doorways, and the walls were adorned with displays of weapons.

Clark stared blankly at the high, vaulted hallway that disappeared into the castle's depths. "I don't suppose you could show me," he asked. "Last time I was here, I got lost trying to find the banqueting hall."

Louis grinned and motioned for Clark to follow him. The blood red carpet covering the flagstones absorbed their footsteps as he led the boy away.

Louis Verne was a qualified chef, and a good one. He'd worked in Metropolis until he was in his midtwenties, serving in several of the city's more prestigious hotels. He liked the irregular hours and the fast pace of city life.

But when he'd broken both legs in a car accident, he moved back to his parents' home in Smallville to recuperate. To his surprise, he'd found that he really appreciated the peace and quiet of the countryside. The big city no longer held any attractions.

When he was ambulant again, he applied for the job as chef at the Smallville Hotel, where he worked for more than a decade.

It wasn't until his parents died, within months of each other, that he began to take stock of his future. He liked his job, he got along fine with the people he worked with, and for such a small town the hotel was actually a pretty classy place. But there had to be more to life.

When he'd seen the advertisement in the vacancies column of the local newspaper, he hadn't hesitated to apply. Lex Luthor, son of a billionaire, would be taking up residence at the mansion. He required a personal chef-cum-butler-cum-personal assistant. A live-in apartment was provided, and extensive foreign travel was a distinct possibility.

The idea of living in a castle, directly responsible to the wealthiest man in town, appealed to Louis.

He got the job.

Now, he led Clark through a carved stone archway into the castle's great hall. A hundred feet long, its vaulted roof supported by massive oak beams, it had a minstrel's gallery running the full width of the wall at the far end. Troubadours had played their bagpipes there, and bards told their tales of good and evil, for generations of Scottish nobility.

A massive stained-glass window took up much of the outside wall. Never part of the original castle, it came from a fourteenth-century French cathedral. Lionel had seen it and liked it. And what Lionel liked, Lionel bought.

They passed through an ornately carved wooden door, and the softly lit corridor suddenly divided into three.

"You go straight on," Louis told Clark. "Third door on the right past the stairs." He himself started to head off down the right-hand hall. "I'm heading for the kitchens. I'll bring you coffee."

❖❖❖

"Penny for them."

Renata tucked her long, shapely legs beneath her and curled up next to Lex on the sofa. Absently, he put an arm around her shoulder, and she leaned her head against his chest.

She'd only been here a couple of days, but it had been long enough for her to realize Lex Luthor seemed to be a changed man. Gone was the hell-raising firebrand she had known and partied with for most of a year. In his place was a new model Lex, colder and more distant, playing his cards close to his chest. What was the word for it?

Inscrutable.

Oh, he'd been pleasant enough to her, and was far from averse to rekindling their relationship. But his passion seemed to have deserted him. At least, where Renata was concerned.

"What are you thinking about?" she tried again.

Lex had been sitting staring into the fire, lost in thought. He looked up at her. Then, as if coming to a snap decision, he started to talk.

"Frankly, I've been wondering why you're here, Renata."

"Darling, I told you—"

"Hear me out," Lex broke in brusquely. "First, you might be here for some kind of shakedown. I give you money, and you don't sell the secrets of our past to the tabloids."

"Lex, how can you say that?" Renata protested. Though, truth be told, it was something she had considered. But a better idea had come along.

"Second," Lex went on, as if she hadn't spoken, "you've maybe realized I'm the only guy for you." He regarded her through half-shut eyes. "Unlikely. Not least because there are plenty richer than me."

Renata sat upright, doing her best to look offended. "You

make me sound like some kind of cheap gold digger," she complained.

"Anything but cheap, darling." Lex smiled. "And thirdly, you might be here because somebody's paying you to spy on me."

For a moment, Renata froze. Had she given herself away in something she'd said or done? But she could think of nothing that might have alerted him.

Of course. It was just Lex playing mind games. Throwing mud at a wall to see what sticks.

She wouldn't rise to his bait. There was no problem.

Relaxing, she leaned back against him, taking his hand in hers and raising it to her lips. "You're just paranoid, darling," she told him. "That's what happens when you live out in the sticks, far from sanity and civilization."

"You're right. As always." Lex slipped his arm around her. "Come here and give me a kiss."

But as their lips met, Lex Luthor was feeling satisfaction rather than passion. Her words were fine, but her body language had given her away.

Renata was a spy.

The corridor had a curve to it so Clark couldn't see the far end, giving him the impression of an endless hallway to nowhere.

In recesses in the walls, antiquities from around the world were displayed. A full set of Samurai armor from seventeenth-century Japan was spotlit, its steel swords and daggers glinting in the light. Ten feet away, a set of Assyrian face masks and chain-mail tunics were fixed to the wall. Next to them was a multicolored Native American headdress and tomahawk. A four-foot-long lead crucifix hung in an archway. Byzantium, Lex had told him, but it meant nothing to Clark.

The overall effect was incongruous, but startling. Like seeing the world's past marching across a stage.

Clark never failed to be awed by his friend's home. The whole Kent farmhouse would have fit inside the great hall alone.

The doorway ahead stood open, and he could see Lex lounging in a leather sofa, a pretty girl draped across his body.

Clark thought maybe he should leave again. But Lex had seen him, and called out, "Hey, Clark. Come on in."

Clark walked into the armory. Though it wasn't cold, a log fire burned in a massive iron grate. Pikes and swords and maces and axes adorned the walls in a series of displays, each one carefully picked out by a soft-sheen spotlight. There were several racks representing firepower through the ages, flintlock muskets, rifles, and single-shot pistols. In the far corner stood a massive cannon—reclaimed, Lex had told him, from a fifteenth-century Spanish galleon that the castle's owners had sunk. In financial straits, they were earning a living as pirates at the time.

Lex and the tall, shapely woman rose to greet him. Clark felt suddenly clumsy and gauche, a fumbling schoolkid compared with these two sophisticates.

It wasn't a new feeling. Lex often had that effect on him. Everything the guy wore was designer-made, though he'd never be so crass as to leave the labels sewn on. He was good-looking, in an unusual sort of way. His hair had never grown back after the day the meteors fell, the day his asthma vanished. But where baldness made some men look thuggish, and others prematurely old, it only added to Lex's un-doubted charisma.

"Clark, I'd like you to meet Renata Meissen. An old . . .

acquaintance." Lex introduced them. "Renata, this is my friend, Clark Kent."

Clark shook Renata's hand. It was cool, and her grip was strong. The heady smell of her musky perfume wafted around her.

Lex certainly knew how to pick his women.

Renata excused herself and left them alone.

"Sit." Lex guided him to an opulent leather armchair. "If you don't mind me saying, you look a little stunned."

"This place always freaks me," Clark admitted. "It makes the Metropolis Museum of Art seem somehow inadequate."

Lex laughed and sat back down on the sofa. "Ever been to Hearst's palace?" When Clark shook his head, he went on. "At San Simeon, in California. Hearst was a newspaper magnate, the richest man in the country, and he built this incredible palace furnished with every treasure money could buy. His dining room came from a medieval monastery. The swimming pool was lined with friezes from a Roman bath." He laughed again. "He even had exotic animals—lions and tigers and zebras—wandering the grounds. At least Dad didn't inflict that on me."

Clark knew there was a lot that Lionel Luthor *had* inflicted on his son. There was no love lost between the two. Nothing Lex did ever satisfied his father. And Lex resented the fact that, although Lionel had planned the castle and its contents down to the last sword and shield, he had never even set foot inside it. It was as if he'd built a luxury prison—then sentenced his own son to live in it.

Lex's face became serious. "The sheriff's deputy called me earlier. He wanted to know if I had a private zoo. Seems they think it was a bear or a wolf that killed Mr. Tait."

Clark shrugged expressively. "It just seems so . . . unlikely."

"No doubt the sheriff will catch it in the end." Lex leaned

toward him suddenly, his voice dropping to a conspiratorial whisper. "Okay, what's the skinny?" he asked. "You and Lana, last night?"

Clark couldn't help but smile. Lex sounded genuinely interested, sincerely excited on his friend's behalf. *Maybe that's another reason I like him so much,* Clark thought. *He's kind of like a big brother.*

"There's nothing to tell," Clark insisted. "We get along swell. I've never been happier. And Lana says she'll come with me to your party."

"Great! You two were destined to be together. You make a great couple. One thing intrigues me, though. What made Lana change her mind?"

Clark frowned. It seemed like everybody was going to ask him the same question that he was asking himself. "I wish I knew," he confessed. "It can't have been my riveting personality or my skills on the sports field."

"Don't put yourself down, pal," Lex urged. "You have hidden depths—as I know better than anyone."

Clark glanced at his friend, careful to keep his face expressionless. He knew what Lex was referring to—the mystery of his sports car with the peeled-back roof. Clark had lied when he claimed the car missed him as it careened off the road and through the bridge parapet. In fact, it had struck him full on. Any ordinary person would have been killed outright, or seriously injured and drowned in the river.

But Clark couldn't tell anyone—not even his best friend—that he was no ordinary person.

That was something else he liked about Lex. The guy was sharp as a razor. Clark always had to be on his toes.

Lex suddenly changed the subject. "Okay, dude. Saturday." He leaned over to the coffee table and picked up a sheaf of handwritten notes. "I've booked a rock band for the great hall. Is that cool? Do kids still listen to rock, or is it all hip-hop and trance nowadays?"

"Not in Smallville," Clark told him. "Rock sounds good to me."

"And I have a conjuror coming. Is that too passé?"

"Could be, if it's rabbits and hats." Clark thought for a moment. "Maybe he could do the same sort of tricks, only with DVDs and skateboards."

"And your folks will be able to provide everything I asked for?"

Clark nodded. "One hundred percent organic. When did Mom and Dad ever let anybody down? They're solid. If they can't make the weight, they'll rope in the neighbors for help."

And that was something else Clark liked about him. Lex believed in thinking global and acting local. Wherever possible, he sourced everything he needed from local businesses. And the Smallville economy needed every boost it could get.

Suddenly, an alarm bell started to ring in the hallway outside, its shrill, insistent tones muted by the carpets and tapestries.

"Probably Louis," Lex guessed, "setting it off by accident."

He slid open a drawer in the bureau against the wall and pulled out an electronic device. He tapped a button, and the monitor screen on his desktop computer flared into life. A schematic of the castle interior appeared on the screen, with a flashing red dot in one corner.

"Yes, it's in the kitchen area. Almost definitely Louis."

He stretched out a hand to grasp the shaft of a medieval, nail-studded mace hanging on the wall. He pulled it free and headed for the exit.

"Best not to take chances," he announced. "You stay here, Clark."

"As if!" Clark muttered, already on his feet and follow-ing his friend.

Louis Verne was busy making two cafe lattes when the alarm went off. It had happened before, a couple of times in the past week alone. Each time, they found a bat had found its way in through one of the narrow slits, and set off the in-truder alarm.

He paid no heed to it, but continued steaming milk on the gleaming, state-of-the-art electric range. Once, these kitchens had boasted spits that would roast a whole ox, and ovens producing hundreds of bread loaves, all for the plea-sure of noblemen and kings.

And on Saturday night, it would be Louis Verne doing the cooking. He had a passion for good food, and he knew it showed in the quality of the meals he produced.

But 120 teenagers equated to about two hundred burgers, and half that in hot dogs. And about a gallon of his home-made relish.

There was a scraping noise behind him, and Louis turned just in time to see the heavy oak door slam closed. Just a draft blowing through the castle's nooks and crannies?

No. Something had come into the kitchen. He was sure of it.

He couldn't see the floor at the far end of the white-tiled room because of the shiny steel cooking ranges between him and the wall. But he could hear a sound as something moved, like a dog's claws tapping on the tiles.

There was a sudden blur of motion. A figure leaped up onto the hood of a gleaming kitchen range. Pots and pans went clattering to the floor as it charged toward Louis, roar-ing like a wild beast.

Only the chef's instincts saved him. He threw himself backward and to the side, and his leg caught against a stack of saucepans. He went down among them with a crash, as the leaping creature sailed over his head.

He scrambled to his feet, heart pounding. The creature had disappeared again, leaping down from the range to dodge behind a massive, catering-size freezer. Louis's fall had brought him close to a wall-mounted rack that held a selection of carving knives and meat cleavers.

Eyes riveted to the big white freezer, he backed toward the knife rack. His hand grasped the handle of a cleaver, quickly bringing it in front of his body.

Whatever this beast was, he'd be ready for it. Damn, he should have heeded the alarm! His eyes scanned the room feverishly, and he strained his ears for the slightest sound. There—at the other end of the kitchen. Louis swiveled his head in time to see a clawed hand swipe into the open electrical junction box.

There was a small explosion of sparks, and then the lights went out.

Clark ran along a tapestry-lined hallway, with Lex a few feet in front.

They'd just turned a right-angled corner, where a stone staircase spiraled up to the left, when the hall was plunged into darkness.

Lex came to an abrupt halt, and Clark skidded into him.

"I guess a fuse has blown," Lex said, "and tripped out the whole house. There's a flashlight in the cupboard halfway up these stairs we passed. Wait here while I go find it."

Clark heard him shuffle toward the wall, no doubt extending his hand for guidance. Then his feet padded away as he began to retrace his steps.

"Help!" There was a cry from someplace up ahead, at the end of the corridor.

"That sounds like Louis," Clark yelled after Lex. "He must be in trouble."

"I've reached the stairs," Lex called back. "I'll be there in a couple of minutes."

Whatever danger Louis is in, Clark thought worriedly, *he might not last a couple of minutes.*

He stared hard in the direction of Louis's voice, his eyes unblinking. His strange, alien vision came into play. Almost like taking an X-ray with his own eyes, he was able to see right through the kitchen wall.

The kitchen was in darkness, but Clark saw a vague skeletal figure backed against the wall. He was waving a cleaver wildly in front of him, trying to hold something at bay. Clark focused on the creature, puzzled that its entire skeleton seemed to be glowing green. It looked like an animal, but it stood on its hind legs.

And it was stalking inexorably toward Louis, stooping low to come in under his frantic lunges with the cleaver.

By the time Lex found the flashlight, it could be all over.

Clark made a snap decision. He accelerated instantly to superspeed. Simultaneously, he kept his vision focused so he could see in the darkness.

A second later the kitchen door loomed ahead. Twisting his body, his shoulder slammed into the door. It almost flew off its hinges as it burst open and crashed against the wall.

Clark came to a sudden halt just inside the doorway, as a wave of fatigue and pain swept over him. Perspiration beaded on his forehead, and he started to shiver uncontrollably. His stomach convulsed. The veins in his wrists and ankles began to expand and contract, feeling like snakes writhing under his skin.

He fell back against a freezer door, leaning there, screwing his eyes up against the nausea and pain that coursed through him.

Only one thing had this kind of effect on him. The meteors.

Something in the makeup of the meteor swarm that accompanied him to Earth was also a deadly toxin to his alien body. He knew that it could affect humans, too—but not in this way. It seemed to change them—mutate their DNA, perhaps—but it didn't kill them.

"Who's there?" He heard Louis's urgent voice from the other end of the room. "Be careful. There's some kind of wild beast in here!"

With all the willpower Clark could muster, he tried to blot out the pain. Something was running toward him, its claws clattering on the polished tile floor. Desperately, Clark focused his eyes. There was a flash as his vision shifted, and he saw the eerie green figure of . . . something. Claws extended, fangs bared, and drooling, it was diving directly at him.

Biting his lip against his distress, Clark balled his fist and punched upward as hard as he could. Pain blazed through his knuckles where his blow landed. The creature yelped and went skidding across the floor.

Clark nursed his hand, trying to soothe the white-hot pain that radiated up his arm.

There was a scrabbling at the doorway, then the creature was gone.

Sighing, Clark sank to his knees and rested his forehead against the freezer door. With the source of the meteor emanations removed, he was starting to recover already.

"Who's there?" Louis called again. "Are you all right?"

"Just about," Clark gasped.

The lights flared back into life, and Lex Luthor stood framed in the kitchen doorway, the mace held like a war club, ready for action.

Even as the lights flickered back into life, Ray Dansk was cursing his luck as he climbed down the rough stonework wall that had given him access to the kitchen windows.

His shoulder hurt like hell, where that interfering brat teenager had hit him.

It had been a stroke of genius, ripping out the kitchen lights. He'd known somehow, in some vague way, that he'd be able to see in the dark. And the instinct was right. He'd seen everything in shades of green, as if through an infrared viewer. Verne had been at his mercy.

And then that clown intervened.

He should have killed them both. He would have, if that bastard hadn't hit him so hard.

He snarled as he leaped down the final six feet, and landed lightly on the close-cut lawn banking that surrounded the castle. His lips drew back over his teeth as he turned to take a final look.

Then he loped off into the undergrowth and became one with the shadows.

He'd failed tonight. But there would be other chances.

Right now, he was going home to lick his wounds.

"How did you find your way to the kitchen in the dark?" Lex demanded.

Clark could only shrug. "Luck, I guess."

They'd quickly ascertained that Louis wasn't hurt, and now the three of them were seated on padded leather stools at the breakfast bar, drinking tea.

"Coffee will just set us on edge," Louis explained. "A smoky China tea will soothe the nerves and calm the mind."

Clark sniffed suspiciously as he raised the cup to his lips. It smelled like it had been smoked, all right. He took a sip and nodded his approval.

"What was that thing, anyway?" Lex asked.

"It was dark. I didn't get a proper look. But it has sharp

claws—" Clark held up his arm, and for the first time the other two noticed his jacket sleeve was badly torn. "I guess it did this when it dived over my head."

Lex looked thoughtful. "It has to be connected with the attack on your schoolteacher the other night. What was his name—Tait?"

"Sheriff Shugrue says it's some kind of wild beast."

"Not so wild that it didn't know ripping out a junction box shuts the power off," Lex pointed out dryly.

"I only got a glimpse of it myself," Louis put in. "It didn't move like a man, believe me. More like a big lizard of some kind. It was real fast. It would have killed me if Clark hadn't interrupted."

"The only lizard I know of that's big as a man," Lex offered, "is the komodo dragon. They can grow to about eight feet long. Adults can eat a goat in one bite."

Lex picked up the wall-mounted telephone and punched in the number for the sheriff's office. "We'd better let the authorities know. File a report, or whatever."

Clark felt Lex's eyes boring into him, but returned the look levelly. He knew what Lex was thinking. *How did Clark get to the kitchen in the dark? How come he didn't break bones busting that door open?*

Clark sighed. Lex already had enough suspicions concerning him and his abilities.

This was the last thing he needed.

"You say it was Luthor's chef who was attacked?" Jonathan frowned at his son. "Isn't that Louis Verne?"

Clark nodded. "Yes, Louis."

Lex had left his details with the deputy on night duty and been assured he'd be contacted next day. Then he'd driven

Clark home—but in his four-by-four, not the silver Porsche, because Louis Verne refused to stay in the castle alone. And there was no way he could squeeze into the rear of the sports car.

Clark invited them both in for a nightcap, but he understood when Lex politely refused. Jonathan Kent wasn't the Luthor family's biggest fan, and he could get pretty crotchety when Lex was around.

He waved from the porch as Lex launched the big German off-roader back into the night.

Now, his father was stroking his chin, deep in thought. "What is it they say?" he asked. "Once is happenstance. Twice is—"

"Coincidence," Martha finished for him.

"And we seem to have quite a coincidence here." Clark looked puzzled, and Jonathan went on. "A guy called Ray Dansk came out to the farm and asked me for a job. That night, Henry Tait was killed. Now, Tait just happened to be a witness at Dansk's trial for manslaughter."

"That's right," Clark agreed. "Chloe looked it up in the records."

Jonathan took a sip from the glass of apple juice on the table by his elbow. "Louis Verne was a witness at the same trial. Now he's been attacked." He frowned at Clark again. "You say it was some kind of beast—and yet your strength couldn't stop it?"

Clark shook his head. "It had the same sort of effect on me as Lana's necklace. Twisted me up inside, jangled every nerve in my body."

"Maybe all it needs is a little human detective work to pull the pieces together," Jonathan said. "I'm going to call Bryan Shugrue."

Clark sighed. "And I'm going to think about getting a lead vest!"

CHAPTER 9

Thursday

"Three! Eleven! Seventeen!"

The football players clustered in a huddle as the team coach yelled his instructions. As one, they broke and ran to their positions.

"Call that running?" the coach snapped, pointing at Pete Ross. "I've seen retired couch potatoes move faster!"

Pete hung his head. Two of his older brothers had been stars of the football team. Much though he wanted to emulate them, he sometimes thought he was more likely to end up winning the title of worst player in school.

The Smallville Crows didn't have a game on the coming Saturday, but they were already practicing for their game the week after. Their opponents would be the Marston Marauders, who were vying with the Crows for top position in the league. It was always one of their hardest games.

And practice wasn't going at all well.

The football curved through the air toward a wide receiver, but he fumbled the pass and the ball went skidding between his legs.

"Where's Whitney?" someone asked dispiritedly.

"I wish I knew," the coach snapped.

Whitney was their star quarterback. To a large extent, the coach had built the entire team around him, with Whitney as the axis that held it all together. But he hadn't shown up for roll call this morning, and now, for the first time ever, he was missing football practice.

"Isn't that him now?" Pete scooped up the ball, and gestured to a lone figure walking slowly toward the field from the direction of the school.

Everyone stopped what they were doing, waiting for Whitney to arrive.

"You're late," the coach told him. "And you haven't changed yet."

As Whitney drew closer, Pete could that his eyes were red-rimmed, and the stubble on his chin was still unshaved.

"I'm sorry, coach," the distraught teenager said miserably. "But I won't be playing today. Or any other day." He stared at the ground, unable to meet the coach's eye. "I quit."

The other players could only stare, dumbfounded, as the coach struggled to find a reply.

Without waiting for any reaction, Whitney slouched back toward the school.

"Have you heard?" Pete asked breathlessly as he dashed into the *Torch* office.

Clark and Chloe were already there, laying out the pages for the next issue.

"Whitney's quit the football team!"

Chloe gazed at the contents plan on her monitor and shook her head irritably. "Blast. Now I have to find something to ditch so we can run the story."

"Listen to the hard-boiled reporter," Pete quipped. "The story comes first—the human tragedy, the loss to a great school team, comes a poor second." He rolled his eyes. "Get with the program, Chloe. Without Whitney, the Marauders will cream the Crows!"

"So why did he quit?" Chloe asked, casting a sharp

glance at Clark. "Too traumatized by his love life to play ball?"

Clark buried himself in his paperwork and remained silent, though he was unable to suppress a twitch of guilt. He'd seen firsthand how badly Whitney was affected by his unexpected breakup with Lana. But nobody could have predicted this.

"It's almost one for the Wall of Weird," Chloe went on. "Whitney loves football nearly as much as he loves himself."

"I guess he loves Lana a whole lot more," Pete commented. He opened the door again, ready to leave. "'Scuse me, guys. I have to go spread the news to the great unwashed."

There was an uncomfortable silence after he left the room. Clark pretended to be busy, ignoring Chloe's questioning look.

"Well, Romeo?" she said at last. "Any comment on Whitney's resignation?"

"I'm sorry about it," Clark said sincerely. "I didn't mean for this to happen—and I'm sure Lana didn't, either."

"You should know," Chloe returned, and he was taken aback by the near-accusing tone in her voice. "The two of you were so wrapped up in each other this morning, you didn't even speak to anyone else."

Clark pushed his papers aside and sighed. "Sorry," he apologized. "I don't mean to offend my friends. It's just—"

"Love," Chloe finished for him.

He felt distinctly uncomfortable as she swiveled her chair until she was facing him. It had occurred to him more than once that Chloe had a secret crush on him. He could never really be sure. If she had, she kept it well hidden.

"Has Lana told you yet why she changed her mind?"

Clark shook his head. "I don't see she needs a specific reason," he said. "Emotion is a fairly uncontrollable thing."

"Spare me, Sigmund." Chloe laughed. "All I know is, Lana went to the gift shop to buy something special for Whitney. She then dumped Whitney the next day—and is no doubt planning to give a certain Clark Kent whatever it was she bought."

Clark considered this for a minute. Chloe was right—it had all happened as quickly as that. He and Lana had been friends for years . . . so what had suddenly happened to change that friendship into passion?

There was one way he might find out, he realized. He could go see Miss Mayfern himself. However unlikely, she might be able to cast light on the mystery.

Aloud, he said, "We should be working, not gossiping."

He leaned across to tap a couple of keys on Chloe's keyboard. The screensaver disappeared, to be replaced by a copy of the *Daily Planet,* a major Metropolis newspaper. The particular edition they were looking at was twelve years old.

"Dad told me last night that Henry Tait and Louis Verne testified against a guy called Ray Dansk." He clicked the mouse with a finger, and the newspaper's front-page feature enlarged to fill the screen. SMALLVILLE MAN JAILED FOR 12 YEARS. There was a grainy photograph of Dansk in hand-cuffs, trying to shield his face from the camera. "Also, according to Dad, Dansk has been released. He turned up looking for a job the other day."

"Hey, I knew I was onto something," Chloe crowed. "It could be some kind of creature this Dansk has trained to attack on command."

"Who knows?" Clark said, noncommittally.

Chloe playfully elbowed him aside. Two clicks on the mouse, and the image altered again. Chloe's face darkened.

"Three witnesses gave evidence against Dansk," she said gravely. "Henry Tait—deceased. Louis Verne—attacked."

She turned away from the screen, and its flickering light played across her face as she looked somberly at Clark. "And Nell Potter."

Clark walked up Durban Street in the late-afternoon sunshine. Already he was wondering what he was doing here. Why had he let Chloe's suspicions get to him? Why couldn't she just accept the fact that Lana loved him, with no enigmatic complications?

But it wasn't fair blaming Chloe. The problem ran deeper. Despite the intensity of his feelings for Lana, he couldn't pretend he was blind to the way she'd behaved. Whitney might be a cheesehead, but, at the very least, he deserved an explanation. And in private, not public.

Lana had been thoughtlessly cruel. And he knew that wasn't like her at all.

But what could Miss Mayfern possibly know of Lana's actions? Maybe better all around if he retraced his steps, went home, and settled for what he always wanted. Lana and him as a couple.

He'd followed the sign on the overgrown lawn, and was at the shop door before he realized there was no going back. For Miss Mayfern was standing inside. She'd drawn back the dusty lace curtain and was staring hard at him.

Clark gulped, and the old lady stood back as he opened the door.

"Hi," he said nervously. "I'm hoping to find a gift for my girlfriend." Which was true. He intended to give Lana something special on Saturday night.

Miss Mayfern glowered suspiciously. "And you are . . . ?"

"Kent, ma'am. Clark Kent. Son of Jonathan and Martha."

The old lady squinted in disbelief, her blue eyes almost vanishing completely into the wrinkled skin around them. "I remember Martha Kent. Couldn't have babies. Near broke her heart."

"I'm adopted, ma'am."

"Aha!" Miss Mayfern sounded as if she'd just solved a difficult puzzle. She pointed to the pair of cane chairs at the table. "Sit. We'll drink some mint tea, and you can tell me all about yourself."

Nell Potter half closed her eyes as she rubbed polish deep into the wood of her hundred-year-old bureau. She loved the sensuous feel of the wood, loved seeing the grain spring into prominence, loved the smell of the beeswax polish she always used.

Of course, her housemaid did everything else. But once a month, this was Nell's special treat. *Sometimes,* she thought, with Handel's *Water Music* playing on the record deck, *life isn't so bad.*

She was alone in her house, the fine six-bedroom country home she'd bought with the money she inherited when her sister Laura died. She'd furnished it well, intent on giving her sister's daughter a decent upbringing. There was a small riding stable a short distance away that came with the house, and a meadow where Lana could ride.

The bureau was worth a lot of money. It had been made by James Lapinski, a Polish immigrant who'd set up home in Smallville at the end of the previous century. A master carpenter, his homemade furniture was now highly collectable. Nell had thought once or twice of shipping it to Metropolis and placing it in one of the big auctions. But somehow she'd never gotten around to it. Maybe the bureau was destined to stay in Smallville forever.

Like me, Nell thought with an uncharacteristic twinge of bitterness. *Destined to grow old in a small town lost in the middle of Kansas, until I become a human antique.*

It hadn't always been like this. Once, the world was her oyster. She was young and pretty, with a head full of smart ideas. She was ambitious and clever and determined. One day, her business empire would straddle the globe. She'd be voted whiz kid of the century. She would franchise abroad, and become Smallville's answer to Nike and Coca-Cola.

Then the meteors fell, and Nell Potter's world came crashing down.

She closed her eyes, remembering. She had been babysitting three-year-old Lana, waiting for Lewis and Laura to get back from the Homecoming Parade. Lana was so cute, pretty as a picture in her sparkling silver dress. She held a magic wand in her hand, practicing for her role as a fairy.

They saw Lewis's car pull up outside, and hurried out to greet them. Then a chunk of flaming rock rained down, and the air was full of smoke and sulfur and fire and explosion. And Laura and her husband were dead.

Nell clutched Lana to her, and let the child wail until sleep finally claimed her.

It was a horror neither of them would ever forget. Nell had immediately abandoned all her own plans and applied to adopt Lana. The little girl was shattered by her parents' death. She didn't know why it had happened. She couldn't understand that, even if she waved her magic wand forever, they could never come back to her.

Lana needed Nell. If she ever felt resentful that she'd become a surrogate mother, that her life was now devoted to bringing up her sister's child, she never showed it. She knew her duty, and she performed it without complaint.

Lana was her daughter now. The child's welfare must always come first.

And so, over the years, Nell Potter's dreams had slowly disappeared. Not died, exactly, for death was swift and sure. It was more that, with the passing of time, her dreams became frayed at the edges and started to unravel. Until eventually they began to dissipate like smoke.

Count your blessings, girl, she told herself now. *You have a beautiful daughter, a nice home, a varied if predictable social life. You play killer canasta. You're still relatively young and pretty.*

And someplace out there, there's a man just for you.

She realized she'd been polishing with a dry cloth for the past minute and reached for the can of furniture polish. The door chimes sounded. Nell wiped her hands, hurriedly took off her apron, and went to the door.

"Nell."

"Bryan Shugrue! You don't often make it this far out of town."

"No trouble this far out, Nell. Not usually, anyhow."

They'd known each other for years. Bryan had even asked her out on a date once, and Nell went. Though as she watched him devour three bags of popcorn during the movie he took her to see, she knew there would never be anything much between them.

"Looking for stolen corn? Somebody's chickens on the road again?"

Sheriff Shugrue smiled, but the humor didn't extend to his eyes. "I wish," he said softly. "Unfortunately, it's something potentially a lot more serious."

Nell frowned, and waited for him to explain.

"You heard about Henry Tait?" he asked, and she nodded.

"We figure he was attacked by an animal. Last night, Louis Verne was attacked out at the Luthor place." Nell nodded again. She'd had at least half a dozen phone calls to give her the gossip. "Nobody got a good look, but it sounds to me like the same animal."

"I'm not sure where you're going with this, Bryan."

The sheriff looked uncomfortable. "Ray Dansk was released from prison this week. He's back in town."

Nell felt a sudden chill course through her. "You think he killed Henry?"

"No, not exactly. But you have to admit it looks suspicious. He comes back, they get mauled. Like he has some sort of trained beast. A bear, maybe. Or tiger."

"In Smallville?" Nell's voice sounded more lighthearted than she felt. "Don't you think somebody might have noticed as he led it up Main Street?"

"I know it sounds silly, Nell. All the same, it's a possibility." His voice became even more serious. "I want you to stay alert. Just in case. If Dansk is shooting for revenge on the folks who testified against him, I don't want you getting hurt."

"Thanks for the warning, Bryan. I'll look out," she promised.

She watched as he lumbered down the porch steps and back to his car, his nightstick and handcuffs clanking against his leg. *Looks like he never stopped eating the popcorn.* A trained bear? She didn't know whether to laugh, or feel terrified.

As he waited for Miss Mayfern to return, Clark studied the shop interior. The shelves were bare. The Lucky Dip barrel was empty. She couldn't possibly make a living from this. Of course, maybe she didn't need to. Maybe she only kept the shop as a way of giving her an interest in life, of staving off the slowdown of old age.

Light glinted off the silver platter Miss Mayfern carried carefully into the shop. She set it down on the table, settled herself in her cane chair, and poured mint tea from the pitcher. Clark watched as the green liquid filled the glasses.

"This will soothe your troubled mind," Miss Mayfern said as she passed him the cup. "Made with mint from my own garden and water from my own well."

Clark felt a sudden twinge of nausea in his stomach that should have alerted him to danger. But unthinkingly, he raised the glass to his lips and took a deep drink.

He gasped as his throat began to burn, the pain spreading at lightning speed down his gullet and into his chest. His stomach cramped, and it was all he could do to put down the glass without dropping it from his shaking hand.

"Are you all right?" Miss Mayfern asked anxiously.

The attack passed as quickly as it had come, leaving him with a dull throb somewhere in his abdomen. He pulled a handkerchief from his pocket and wiped perspiration from his brow.

"I just felt dizzy for a moment there. I'm fine now."

"Good. Before I can match you with the perfect gift, I have to know all about you." Her blue eyes fascinated him. "So tell me."

Clark felt light-headed, his thoughts vague and wispy. He furrowed his brow, trying to concentrate. For some reason, he couldn't quite remember why he'd come here.

Instead, he found himself pouring out his heart to the old lady, who nodded and clucked and pursed her lips.

Like a bird, he thought. *Like a wise old bird.*

"Sometimes, I find myself envying the other kids." Clark heard himself speaking, but somehow his vocal cords no longer needed any input from his mind. He was talking without thinking, dredging up stuff that he usually tried to stifle. "I mean, they have such normal lives. It must be great."

"You're not normal?" the old lady prompted.

"Not really. I feel like an alien. As if everybody else in Smallville has their part to play in the grand scheme of things." He paused, his voice sinking as sadness welled up in his heart. "Except me. I don't belong. I'm different."

Miss Mayfern tutted understandingly. "Every teenager feels that way. It's just a phase. You'll find your place one day."

"I don't think so. There will never come a day when I can look around me and feel that I belong." He raised his hand to massage his temples, then ran it through his dark hair. "I'm just . . . not normal."

"You listen to me, Clark Kent," the old lady said fiercely. She leaned toward him, those piercing blue eyes like a magnet he couldn't resist. He felt himself falling, his whole perception spiraling around him. "You're as normal as anyone else. We're all the same. No human is worth more than another. We're all the same. All normal.

"And you are, too, Clark Kent. Just the same as everyone else, a normal teenager, like all of your friends."

It was another half hour before Clark left Miss Mayfern's.

His dizziness had gone, and the throb in his gut, but his thoughts were still confused and unfocused. He looked down the hill toward downtown, and felt a sudden thrill of pleasure.

Smallville! he thought joyfully. *My home.*

He ambled past the old chestnut tree, its majestic branches mottled with color as the sun set behind it. For a moment, he felt an affinity with that tree, some special bond that linked the two of them together. It was a Smallville tree, and he was a Smallville kid.

He felt like bursting into song. He felt so good, he could almost fly.

He was home. And he loved it.

CHAPTER 10

Thursday night

"What did the sheriff have to say about Ray Dansk, Dad?"

"The guy tried a whole string of places at the start of the week, looking for work. But nobody's seen hide nor hair of him since."

Jonathan and Clark were walking across the yard behind the house. The moon was out, but a line of dark clouds swept across its face. Jonathan could feel the night breeze through the sleeves of his checked cotton shirt, cooler than it had been for a while now.

"Storm belt's moving down from the northwest," he announced. "It'll probably take a couple of days to get here."

"Oh, great. Just in time for Lex's party."

They passed the coops where the chickens were caged for the night, their soft clucking sounding like curious questions as father and son walked by. At the door of the old barn, Jonathan reached inside to flick on the power lamps that lit the interior.

Inside, on the straw-strewn floor, the small tractor was lined up under a mechanical winch. A chain ran down to hook around the tractor's engine. Jonathan nodded toward it.

"I want to use it tomorrow, out on the river field. It's small enough not to sink in the marshy ground. But the engine needs a thorough overhaul." Jonathan patted the chain, which was loose where it ran around the pulley wheel and connected to the winch. "Think you could lift it for me? It would sure save me a lot of valuable time."

A strange look crossed Clark's face, a mixture of incredulity and skepticism. "You're joking, Dad. Right?" Clark tapped the tractor's engine casing lightly. "I couldn't winch this."

Jonathan frowned at him. This wasn't the sort of thing Clark usually joked about. "I understand if you're too busy, son. I just thought—"

"Not too busy, Dad. Too weak. That thing must weigh a couple of hundred pounds. Even Whitney would have trouble shifting it."

"Won't you try?" Jonathan suggested thoughtfully. "For me."

"Sure. But don't say I didn't warn you."

Clark leaned forward and grasped the handle of the winch. The chain tautened. Straining with all his might, he tried to turn the handle farther and start to raise the tractor engine. The veins knotted in his forehead, and he broke out in a sweat as he fought to exert all of his strength. But the winch didn't move another inch.

Clark released his grip on the handle, and the chain went slack again. "Phew, Dad. You must think I'm some kind of superboy."

"Aren't you?" Jonathan asked sharply.

"Chance would be a fine thing." Clark grinned. "Maybe then I'd get on the football team."

"Clark! Clark—telephone!"

Martha Kent's voice broke in on them, coming toward them from the house.

"See you later, Dad."

Clark began to run toward his mother, and met her halfway across the yard.

"Hey, that was slow," she chided. "Usually you're there before I've even left the porch."

Clark looked blankly at her, then took the cordless phone from her hand. Holding it to his ear, he walked off toward the house.

"What was all that about?" Martha asked, as Jonathan came up to join her. His forehead was furrowed as he attempted to make sense of his conversation with Clark.

"I'm not sure," he told his wife grimly. "And I'm not sure that I like it."

"Clark? Pete."

"Yo. To what do I owe the honor?"

"Chloe and I were talking to Lana on the bus home tonight. She's real worried, Clark. She called her aunt on her cell phone—and guess what?"

"Don't keep me hanging, Pete."

"Sheriff Shugrue has advised Nell Potter to be on the alert. He seems to think she could be the next victim of the 'phantom beast,' as Chloe calls it."

"I take it you have a plan?"

"We've arranged to meet up at Lana's. We'll keep them company tonight. Fancy coming along?"

"Wild horses wouldn't stop me. On my way!"

"I just don't get it, Martha. He told me point-blank that he had no superpowers."

"Teenagers can have a strange sense of humor sometimes," Martha told her husband. They were sitting at the big pine table in the kitchen, enjoying a cup of coffee hot from the range. "Remember how you used to laugh at *Monty Python*."

"This is different. He wasn't joking. I asked him to try to

lift the tractor engine." Jonathan shook his head, as if he still couldn't quite believe it. "I saw the effort he put into it. He tried, and he tried, but he couldn't budge it."

"It does seem strange," Martha admitted. "I mean, it's only a small thing, but he *always* uses superspeed when I answer his calls for him."

"The worst of it is, he didn't seem to know he *has* any powers. Almost as if he's totally forgotten about ever having them."

"Who knows?" Martha said quietly. "Maybe that would be a blessing in disguise."

"Another worry, is what it is," Jonathan growled. He took another sip of coffee, but didn't even taste it as he swallowed.

His mind was on his boy.

Renata emerged from the doorway leading to the castle battlements and shivered. *It's chilly up here.* She wished she'd thrown a sweater over her thin silk blouse.

Lex was standing about ten yards away. He had his back to her, elbows resting on the battlement parapet, staring up at the moon. It was almost full tonight, though dark clouds periodically obscured its face.

She made her way over to him, taking care that her shoes' high heels didn't catch in the cracks between the flagstones. Throwing her arms around him, she pressed herself into his back in an attempt to warm her chilled flesh.

"Aren't you cold?" she asked him.

Lex shook his head without turning. "It's a beautiful night. Just look at that sky!"

Renata glanced up. Clouds. A moon.

Unimpressed, she shivered again, and Lex spun around

to face her. "Hey, you're really feeling it, aren't you?" Gallantly, he slipped off his black silk jacket and draped it around her shoulders. "Better?"

Renata nodded. She really liked him when he was like this, tender and concerned and thoughtful. But they'd spent almost a whole year together, off and on. She knew that he had another side to his personality: When the mood was on him, he could be cold, and distant, and utterly ruthless. Lex Luthor was his father's son, and though he might not admit it, he had inherited Lionel's driving ambition and total confidence in himself.

Renata didn't like what she was going to do. But she'd already been paid, so she had no real choice.

"Lex," she said diffidently, "remember what you were saying—about me having an ulterior motive for being here?"

It was as if a hood had been pulled down over his eyes, so she could no longer see any expression there. "Yes."

"Well, you were right," she admitted. "I have a proposition to put to you. A business proposition," she added hurriedly.

"I'm all ears."

Renata pulled his jacket more tightly around her shoulders. "Not here," she said, her teeth almost chattering. "Let's find someplace warm."

Funny, Ray Dansk was thinking, *the cave isn't so bad. In fact, I like it here. Maybe it could be my headquarters. Just like the Dragons, in the old days. Ha, that would be something. SMALLVILLE DRAGONS BRING REIGN OF TERROR TO CORNBALL COUNTY!*

He laughed out loud, then broke off abruptly, unable to

remember what he was laughing at. The echoes seemed to
take forever to die away in the darkness.

Somewhere over in the corner, Henry Tait's head still lay.
It no longer frightened him the way it had. In fact, he was
starting to suspect that *it* was afraid of *him*. It hadn't spoken
in a long time. It was obviously staying out of his way.

Dansk laughed again, until his throat rasped and he began
to cough. Using both hands, he scooped up some water from
the cavern floor and slurped it greedily. He liked it. It didn't
taste like water at all. Water didn't make your mouth tingle
and allow you to see in the dark. Water didn't make the tattoo on your chest writhe like a living thing.

Water didn't nourish you or make you stop smoking. He
hadn't had a cigarette in . . . a long time.

Water didn't *infect* you.

Every now and again, he thought he could make out faint,
wispy tendrils of green mist. Or was it red? Red and angry?

Who cared?

He squatted on his heels, rocking gently back and forth,
laughing softly to himself.

"So. Your proposition . . . ?"

They were snuggled up close together on the leather
couch in the armory, bathed in the warmth radiating from
the log fire, sipping brandy from balloon glasses. Lex's arm
was around her, and Renata found herself momentarily re-
gretting that things hadn't worked out better between them.
There were a lot of fates worse than spending your life with
a man like Lex Luthor.

She shook off the thought. She'd never been one for han-
kering after what might have been. To survive in this jungle

of a world, you did what you had to do. Your only allegiance was to yourself.

"I'll be totally up front," she promised him. "All you have to do is say yes or no."

"I'm listening."

She told him her story, keeping it to the bare essentials. How Carlos, the Colombian she used to score her cocaine from in Metropolis, had come to her with a plan. He'd made some hot connections, at a very high level in the smuggling business. For an investment of one million dollars, she would earn back ten times the amount. And all within a month.

When she finished, the long silence was broken only by the crackling of the fire.

"You're asking me to finance a drug deal?" Lex said at last. His voice was neutral and gave her no hint of what he might be thinking. Or feeling.

"No. I'm asking you to loan me a million. I'll pay back double, within thirty days. A straightforward business arrangement."

"And because it's you doing the deal, that absolves me of any moral responsibility?"

"Something like that."

Lex looked hard at her, but her gaze didn't flinch.

"You know I don't approve of drugs, Renata."

"But you do approve of money."

Lex leaned back, disengaging his body slightly from hers. *Damn,* she thought. *I've blown it. I've lost him.*

But he pursed his lips and narrowed his eyes. "Let me sleep on it."

CHAPTER 11

Thursday night

It's like a morgue in there. As if everybody's waiting for me to be attacked!

Nell Potter poured four large glasses of apple juice and put them on a tray. She tugged open the refrigerator door to replace the juice bottle and glanced through the service hatch that gave access from the kitchen to the lounge.

A cheery fire was blazing in the hearth. Pete Ross and Chloe Sullivan sat together on the sofa, staring into the flickering flames. Clark sat in the big armchair, with Lana perched on the arm beside him, her hand resting on Clark's shoulder.

Teenagers. Nell shook her head. *A year of Whitney, then wham! bam! it's hello Clark.*

Truth was, things weren't much different in her day. Hormones are pretty consistent from generation to generation.

She picked up the tray and forced a bright smile onto her lips as she carried it through to the lounge and offered each of them a glass.

"Store-bought," she said apologetically, as Clark reached to take his. She knew that the Kents still maintained a small orchard, and Martha collected and pressed the apples every autumn.

Nell felt suddenly older than her years, completely out of place among these kids less than half her age. They inhabited a different world. They might as well be an alien species for all the conversation she'd had out of them tonight.

"I'll leave you to your own devices," she told them, suppressing the relief she felt. "I have my monthly accounts to balance. It might take me a while."

"If you need some help—" Clark began, starting to rise.

But Nell held up her hand, palm out. "Thanks for the offer. But I have my own arcane system, and woe betide any outsider who comes in and meddles!"

All four gave an audible sigh of relief as Nell left the room.

It wasn't that they didn't like her, or resented her presence. It was just—as Clark remembered Chloe saying—"Adults come from a different world. They don't understand us, and we don't understand them."

"Do you really think this beast will attack my aunt?" Lana asked when she was sure Nell was out of earshot.

Clark reached up to cover her hand gently with his, and gave it a reassuring squeeze. "Personally, I don't. Not with us around," he said. "The main reason I'm here is because it's a chance to spend time with you."

He felt pressure on his hand as Lana squeezed back. Out of the corner of his eye, he saw Chloe pretending to throw up in an imaginary barf bag.

"I'm not so sure," Pete said slowly, slouched with his feet splayed out, as if he really wanted to put them up on the coffee table. "Clark and Luthor's chef were lucky to escape unhurt. And Mr. Tait was ex-military. He kept himself fit. But this thing managed to rip him to shreds." He grimaced. "And they still haven't found his head!"

"Thanks for reminding us." Chloe elbowed Pete in the ribs. "Lighten up, Ross. That kind of talk is just going to spook the horses. And me. As typical teenagers, we should be gossiping in anticipation of the party on Saturday."

Clark drained the last of his apple juice and set the glass

down on the table. "If it's a flop, it won't be Lex's fault. He's gone to a lot of trouble and expense to get things right."

"Why? That's what I want to know," Chloe said darkly. "I mean, he's at least six years older than us. He's rich as Rockefeller—at least, his father is. He could be partying in New York, or on the French Riviera. Why throw a bash for the teenagers from the back of beyond?"

"Because he's a nice guy," Clark defended his friend. "He really wants to settle in here, to become part of Smallville life. Everybody seems to hate his dad—"

"With good reason," Pete interrupted bitterly. "The man's a liar. My dad and uncle would never have sold the corn factory if he'd told them he was converting it to a fertilizer plant."

"—and probably with good reason," Clark went on, deferring to Pete. "But none of us should be judged according to who our parents are."

"You're right," Pete agreed, a little shamefaced. "I hardly know Lex, but I've never seen anything to suggest he's the same kind of rat as his dad. Just don't tell *my* dad I said that!"

"My father says he's not a bad boss," Chloe said. Her father was plant manager at the LuthorCorp fertilizer plant. "Fair pay, better-than-average health benefits. He says Lex spends time on the factory floor, learning rather than spying."

"He's a very astute businessman," Clark assured them. "Lionel Luthor might have closed that plant down by now if Lex hadn't managed to turn it around."

There was a lull in the conversation. Clark tossed a fresh log onto the fire and bedded it down with the iron poker. A stream of sparks wafted up the chimney. Holding Lana's hand in his, he stared into the flames, seeing faces and landscapes appear and disappear in their flickering form. The only sound was their quiet breathing, the crackling of the flaming log, and the loud tick of a grandfather clock that stood in a corner.

"Did you hear that?" Pete shot upright on the sofa.

"What?"

"I thought I heard a noise outside."

"I didn't hear anything."

"What kind of noise?"

"I'm not sure. Just a noise. Like a noise that I didn't expect to hear. A *noise,* you know?"

Chloe screwed up her eyes and glared. "If this is your idea of a joke, Ross," she began threateningly, but Pete shook his head.

"It's not. I swear. I did hear something."

"Aunt Nell?" Lana called, an edge of anxiety in her voice. "Are you all right?"

Nell Potter walked into the room. "Why? Shouldn't I be?"

"Pete thought he heard something outside," Clark explained. "If you want, we'll go take a look."

Nell raised her eyebrows. "What—and spook yourselves some more?" She picked up her car keys from the mantel. "It's getting late. If you've finished your drinks, I think I'd better take you home."

Suddenly, there was a sound of smashing glass from the rear of the house.

"That was Lana's bedroom window," Nell gasped, her face suddenly ashen.

Clark stood up and hurried over to the door that led into the hallway. "Come on, Pete," he urged. "We'd better check this out."

But Nell pushed in front of them, snatching up the iron poker from where it lay in the fireplace. "This is my house," she reminded them, "and I'm the responsible adult here. I'll check it out myself."

Quietly, she slipped out into the hallway. She stepped over the basket of cleaning materials that lay on the floor. She'd been polishing earlier, and hadn't gotten around to putting everything away when Lana's friends arrived.

She half raised the poker, ready to strike.

Clark and Pete were close behind, with Lana and Chloe bringing up the rear. Nell put a finger to her lips and moved soundlessly toward the stairs leading up to the bedrooms.

"I don't like this, Ms. Potter," Clark whispered. "Please, let Pete and me go first."

Barely had he placed his foot on the first stair, when something flew through the air and smashed into the hall light. Shards of glass from the lightbulb showered down on them, as the hallway and stairs were plunged into darkness.

Light from the lounge spilled out, illuminating the five of them. But, blocked by the wall, the stairs above were shrouded in shadow.

There was a deep roar from the landing above, and something launched itself from the top stair.

"Look out!"

Clark just had time to yell a warning, before the dark form came down heavily on top of him. Instinctively, he tried to squirm away as claws slashed at him. He felt his shirt rip from neck to waist, and a throb in his arm as if he'd been punched.

He tried to lash out against whatever was attacking him, but his assailant retaliated with a punch that took Clark square on the jaw. His head jerked back and slammed into the wall behind him.

His vision seemed to explode with stars, and he slumped forward onto the stairs, unconscious.

"Get back! Into the lounge!" Nell shouted, trying to herd Pete, Lana, and Chloe away from the danger.

She'd had a reputation as a firebrand in her youth, and it took a lot to frighten her. She whirled to face the intruder, swinging the poker as hard as she was able.

The heavy implement whacked into flesh, and the creature gave a shriek of pain. But Nell's satisfaction was short-lived, as the beast lashed out again and sent the poker flying from her hand, nearly breaking her wrist in the process.

"Aunt Nell!" Lana screamed from the lounge, and there was no mistaking the terror in her voice. "Run!"

Defenseless, Nell turned to flee. But her foot caught against the cleaning basket, knocking it over, sending its contents spilling across the hall floor. As Nell lost her balance, she tried to stop her fall by pushing her hands against the wall. But her efforts were in vain, and she crashed to the floor.

Immediately, the beast was on her. She felt its weight on her back as it knelt on her. A clawed hand grabbed her hair and hauled her head back with incredible strength.

This was it, Nell knew. There was no way she had the strength to fight this thing off. It was going to kill her, and poor Lana would be motherless again.

"Lana," she shouted, mustering all of her energy. "Save yourselves! Get outside! Take the car!"

She felt something sharp against her throat, and her whole life started to flash before her eyes . . .

When Pete saw Clark fall to the stairs, he tried to get close enough to pull his friend away. But Nell had shoved him and the girls back through the lounge door.

Now, he gasped as he saw the shadowed form stoop over Nell. It seemed to be human, but its skin had a greenish tinge. It was drooling from its fanged mouth, its bestial eyes flaring as it raised a clawed hand high.

Behind him, in the lounge, Chloe was trying to comfort Lana, who was screaming hysterically.

He had to do something—but what?

He saw the poker lying at the far end of the hallway. Perhaps if he was able to shoulder the beast aside, he could reach it, and—

Plucking up his courage, he took a step forward, and felt his foot kick against something. A plastic bottle of bleach. It started to roll away from him, and he almost dived to grab it. Fingers fumbling, he struggled to unscrew the safety cap.

The beast's claws started to descend in a long, raking arc that would slice into Nell Potter's face and rip out her throat.

"Yaaaaahhh!" Pete leapt forward, yelling as loudly as he could.

The beast looked up, and Pete's resolve almost wavered as he gazed into the depths of its fiery eyes. There was something primeval about them, something alien. With not a trace of humanity.

Then he squeezed the bleach bottle as hard as he could with both hands.

A thick jet shot from the spout, spraying out like a curtain in the air. It spurted full in the beast's face, filling its eyes and nose and slavering mouth with the powerful domestic bleach.

It roared and screamed, both at the same time, and stumbled upright.

Before Pete could step back beyond its reach, its hand swung out and slashed against his face. Pete staggered back. The blow had only grazed him, and it hadn't hurt, but Pete felt blood welling up all across his cheek. Stunned by the realization that he was hurt, he didn't even see the second blow.

The claw came ripping upward from his belly, raking deep as it sliced toward his chest.

Pete collapsed to the floor without a sound.

Clark's vision swam, and there was a ringing in his ears as he regained consciousness and tried to force himself to his feet. A dark shape shambled toward him, backlit by the lounge lights.

He fell back to avoid it.

But the creature didn't even seem to realize he was there. Moaning and yelping, it blundered down the hall, rubbing at its eyes. It rebounded off the wall and knocked over a small table laden with family photographs and mementos.

It clattered through the door onto the rear porch. Glass shattered as it fell against the picture window, then it was scrambling outside.

It lurched into the garden shrubbery, and disappeared from view.

"Lana?" Clark called. His heart had almost stopped beating. Surely that monster couldn't have—

"We're all right," he heard Chloe answer.

Clark sighed with relief as the girls came out of the lounge. Nell Potter was already getting to her feet, shocked but relatively unscathed. Lana ran to embrace her.

"Aunt Nell," she sobbed. "I thought—I thought—"

"So did I, honey," Nell said gently, hugging Lana to her. "But it's all right. I'm shaken up, but apart from a sore wrist, I don't think I'm hurt."

Clark knelt beside Pete, who hadn't stirred since the creature struck him. "Pete?" he whispered hoarsely. There was no reply.

His heart sank as he saw blood oozing from the deep weals that crossed Pete's upper body. His breathing was shallow and labored.

Taking his hand, Clark felt for a pulse. It was weak and irregular.

"Quickly," he shouted. "Call 911. Pete's hurt bad!"

CHAPTER 12

Friday morning

"How is he, Clark?"

Martha looked intently at her son as he replaced the telephone in its cradle on the kitchen wall. Clark bit his lip, and she knew immediately that the news wasn't good.

"Unconscious, but stable," Clark reported miserably. He sat down at the table, resting his head in his hands. "No vital organs were damaged, but he lost a lot of blood."

Pete had been rushed to Smallville Medical Center, where he was placed in the intensive care unit. Clark and Chloe had wanted to go with him in the ambulance which had arrived within minutes of Nell Potter's emergency call. But Sheriff Shugrue had turned up, too, and, after putting out an all-points bulletin, he insisted on them remaining at Nell's. He wanted their statements while the details were fresh in their minds.

It was almost two in the morning before Clark had arrived home, to find his mother and father sitting waiting for him, white-faced with worry. He was bruised and aching, and he had a pounding headache. His shirt hung off him in tatters, but he was otherwise unhurt.

He apologized for not phoning, explaining that in all the excitement it had slipped his mind. He hadn't wanted to leave Lana, but the sheriff insisted she was safe with him.

On top of that business about his superpowers, Martha had been worried sick.

"I'm just glad you weren't hurt," she told Clark now. "I thought—"

But she couldn't tell him what she thought. Though she and Jonathan had happily adopted Clark, and he had been their son for a dozen years, they had no idea what kind of society he originally came from. Superficially, Clark's people must have been very similar to humans. But there was no way they could ever have the boy examined by a doctor, because his incredible powers would undoubtedly be revealed.

What if losing his powers was natural—something every one of his race went through? What if he became progressively weaker from now on, as he lost his normal human powers, too?

What if his parents were some insect-like species, who spun a cocoon when they reached puberty? Only to emerge later as . . . what?

These were the thoughts that had filled Martha's head during those long hours they spent waiting. She hadn't even confided them to Jonathan, though she suspected he might be thinking along similar lines. They'd known from the start their son was an alien. But just what *kind* of alien was he?

"This beast that attacked you," Jonathan asked. "Was it the same one at Lex's castle?"

"I'm pretty sure it was. Like some kind of giant lizard, or something."

Martha shivered. The cup of coffee in her hand had gone cold, but she felt no urge to replace it with a fresh cup. All she could think about was Clark and the awful events unfolding in their town.

"I'm going to take another shower," Clark said. "Maybe it'll soothe these bruises."

Martha waited until he'd gone, then turned to her husband. "How could he be bruised?" she asked, already knowing he had no answer. "My goodness, when I think of the way he was hit by Lex Luthor's car, and came out of it without even a scratch! How can he possibly be bruised?"

Jonathan shook his head, as bewildered as his wife. "It's beyond me. All I can think of is, it must have something to do with the meteorites. We know that he gets real sick if he comes into contact with them."

"But he didn't get real sick," Martha protested. "He said he felt fine, except for a headache and his bruises." She threw her hands wide, incomprehension etched on her face. "The boy can smash brick walls with his head. How can he have a *headache*?"

"What bothers me most is that he doesn't seem to know he ever had any special abilities. How do you just *forget* you can run at sixty miles an hour?"

"Have you asked him about it?"

"Not outright." Jonathan considered for a few seconds. "But maybe that's exactly what I should do."

Bryan Shugrue had wakened with a crick in his neck.

He'd spent the night at Nell's house, sitting with his gun in his hand, on guard in case the mystery attacker returned. Fortunately, it hadn't, because at some point he must have dozed off, his head lolling uncomfortably against a cushion on the sofa.

He started when he heard footsteps coming downstairs and tried to clear his sleep-vague thoughts before Nell and her niece came into the room. They'd spent the night in Nell's room, because Lana's bed and floor were covered in shards of glass.

"I didn't sleep a wink," Lana was saying. "I spent half the night hiding behind the curtains, peeking out the window."

"No need for that," the sheriff said, patting his gun. "I told you I'd stand guard."

"What are we going to do, Aunt Nell? It might come back!"

"I don't know, Lana," Nell admitted. "I just don't know. I've never seen anything like that—that *thing*."

"You can leave all that to me." Sheriff Shugrue leaned against the sofa arm and pushed himself to his feet, his handcuffs clanking against his nightstick. "I'll sort something out until we manage to catch it. Meantime"—he patted his paunch unselfconsciously—"what's for breakfast?"

Jonathan was standing by the refrigerator when the kitchen door clicked open, and Clark came back into the room.

"Here," Jonathan called. "Catch!"

He tossed four eggs through the air toward his son.

Clark looked startled, and hesitated for a split second. Belatedly, he made a futile attempt to catch the eggs. One broke against his hand, while the others splatted against the breakfast bar, leaving long smears as they dribbled to the floor.

Martha stared at her husband in astonishment.

Clark wiped his hand, then looked at his father. "Don't tell me—the yoke's on me."

But Jonathan Kent wasn't smiling.

"What would you say," he asked grimly, "if I told you that up until a few days ago, you'd have caught those eggs at superspeed long before they hit the floor?"

Clark looked skeptical, then gave an exaggerated nod. "Sure, Dad, of course I would. Just like I would have lifted that tractor engine last night, right?"

"You really don't remember?"

Clark heaved a deep sigh. "Dad, I remember this: I'm a

normal guy. I lead a normal life. I have normal friends." He paused, looking from one parent to the other. "The only thing *not* normal is my parents, who seem to think I'm some comic book character."

"That's not fair, Clark," Martha protested. "We're worried about you, that's all."

"Then answer me this," Clark demanded. "Aren't you *happy* with a normal son?"

"Yes!"

"Of course!"

His parents spoke together.

"We love you however you are, Clark," Martha assured him. "But—there seem to be a lot of strange things happening lately. Terrible things. You've been attacked twice. Your friend's in the hospital. Your teacher is dead. We just don't understand what's happening."

"Me neither," Clark muttered. "You see bloodshed and violence on the television, in the movies. But when it gets real—like it did for Pete last night—you just want to be sick."

He slumped down at the table with his head in his hands.

"I'll call your principal," Jonathan said, "and tell him you won't be in school today. Then I'll drive you over to the hospital to see Pete."

"Thanks, Dad." Clark looked up, and smiled ruefully. "You're maybe a bit weird at times, but I wouldn't change you for the world."

Dansk could still taste the foul bleach in his mouth. It seemed to seep out of his very flesh, out of his clothing, until it filled the whole cave and made it stink like a hospital.

He'd spent half the night on his knees, retching, as the

corrosive liquid he'd swallowed attacked his stomach and intestines. His eyes felt like they were full of grit, and his vision was blurred. His fingernails were torn and bleeding, and his tongue throbbed where he'd bitten it in his distress.

He leaned forward, bending his head close to the cave floor. His tongue snaked out between his lips, and he lapped up the cool water like a dog. Cupping his hands, he scooped some up and splashed it over his face, knuckling it into his eyes. If the water really did have unnatural powers, he needed them now.

God alone knew how he'd made it back to the cave. Bent double with pain, hardly able to see, he'd staggered through the night, trying to keep to the shadows. Only instinct had guided him home, back to the cool darkness and its nourishing water.

For a while during the night, he'd thought he was going to die. He didn't mind too much. It seemed perfectly natural. He lay on the floor in the fetal position, spasming and vomiting bile that burned his throat as badly as the bleach had. His mind churned with curses, and jolts of pain, and half-formed thoughts of a terrible revenge.

The hours went by, and his body felt better.

But his mind felt worse.

As if he had acquired a sixth sense, he knew it was morning outside. No matter how bad he felt, he had to leave here at once. The whole idea of abandoning his cave—his home, his womb—filled him with uneasy dread.

But he knew the cops would come back. They'd failed to find him once. They'd have every unit alerted for twenty miles around. They'd bring in dogs and hunt him down like an animal.

Ray Dansk had things to do before that happened.

He took a long, final sip of water from the pool, then rubbed his face with his wet hands.

His fingernails felt almost healed, and the swelling in his tongue had subsided.

This was the best infection he'd ever had.

Carefully, he groped around the cavern floor until he found what he was looking for. Henry Tait. He grabbed the head by the hair and swung it hard. It slammed into the slimy wall with a wet thump.

Ray Dansk's laughter echoed in the foul air as he swung, and swung, and swung.

He looks so small, Clark thought. *Like all the life has gone out of him, and it's just a shell that's left.*

He stood in the small private hospital ward, looking down at his friend in the iron-framed bed. Half of Pete's face was hidden by the respirator that was regulating his breathing. His left arm was hooked to an intravenous drip, and his bare torso was swathed in bandages and dressings. A half dozen monitors recorded his life functions.

You live your life, one day the same as the next, and the next, and the next. Then reality—or a strange, unidentifiable beast—hits you like a sledgehammer.

Beside Clark, Lana and Chloe stood in similar silence, lost in their own thoughts.

Tragedy's something that happens to other people . . . until it happens to you.

There were tears in Lana's eyes as she sat down on the bedside chair and took Pete's unresponsive hand in hers.

"Thanks, Pete," she whispered. "You saved Aunt Nell's life." Pete's eyes remained closed, his breathing steady as the respirator pumped his lungs. "I'm so sorry that it turned out like this. Please . . . please be all right."

Clark saw Chloe's eyes mist over at Lana's words, and he had to blink a tear that pricked at his own.

"Pete was strong when he had to be," he said softly. "Now he needs us to be strong for him."

Dansk slunk out of the main cave and walked slowly toward the chinks of light penetrating the barrier boards. He squinted until he became used to it; his vision was bad enough without blinding himself with sunlight.

As soon as his eyes were acclimatized, he slid out from under the bottom board. He hastily scooped soil and stones into the depression and smoothed it out with his hand.

He peered around suspiciously, seeing the trees and bushes and grass, but no people. He heard a dog barking on the far side of the park, but it was out of his sight.

He stole down through the bushes and weeds to the river-bank. Now that his sight was fully returned, he noticed that his leather jacket and jeans were ripped and torn, and streaked with dried blood. His boots were caked with mud, and there was a long streak of white down one leg of his jeans, where the fabric had been bleached.

He emerged from behind a bush growing on the very lip of the riverbank, and again scouted all around him. The dog's barking was farther away now.

Satisfied, Dansk slipped into the swirling waters.

The river was seven or eight feet deep in the center, but if he stayed close to the bank, it was shallow enough for him to wade along, up to his chest in water. He used one hand to cling to branches and tufts of grass, now and again letting the current carry him as he made his way downstream.

The river water was cold, but he didn't mind. It was like drifting in some cold, cold womb.

Pausing to rest under the branches of an overhanging tree, he tilted his head back to look up the side of the bluff. It was only fifty or so feet high, but from his perspective it looked massive, blotting out the cloudy sky. Atop it, silhouetted against the churning clouds, the old Gothic house seemed to grab at the sky.

Suddenly, he remembered something. He felt in his jacket pocket and pulled out a crumpled piece of wet card. Smoothing it out as best he could, he struggled to read the water-blurred print.

LEX'S PARTY! SATURDAY NIGHT! BRING A FRIEND!

He'd found it lying on a dresser in the bedroom at the Potter place.

He grinned to himself, an ugly leer twitching the corners of his mouth. He dropped the card in the water and watched the current whisk it away.

It was a long time since he'd played the party animal.

Tomorrow's promised to be a zinger.

It was almost 10 A.M. when two police patrol cars roared into Riverside Park, sirens blaring. They screeched to a halt where the road gave out, smoke spewing from their tires.

Led by a grim Bryan Shugrue, clanking as he walked, three deputies carrying tire irons and flashlights hurried along the path that led to the caves. The sheriff had at last taken Jonathan Kent's warning seriously. Three witnesses—three attacks. Ray Dansk had to be involved.

Shugrue remembered that Dansk had led a motorcycle gang for a short while. The Smallville Dragons. They were troublemakers, small-time hoodlums who wanted to be big-time hoodlums but never would be. Banned by almost every bar and diner in town, they used to hang out at the cave beneath the Durban Street bluff.

He'd already ordered two of his deputies to check it out a couple of days earlier, but they'd reported back to say the barriers hadn't been tampered with. Half the police in the county were now looking for Dansk, but so far without success. Nobody had seen him for days. Was it possible he was hiding out at his old stamping ground?

Only a proper search would determine that.

Shugrue was puffing breathlessly by the time they reached the boarded-up entrance. He stood back to catch his breath as his men used their tire irons to pry the boards apart, then lever them off. The nails gave with shrieks of tortured metal and groaning wood.

"Morrison—Martin—shine those flashlights inside."

The powerful beams lit up the cave's interior. Near the entrance, thick green moss festooned the walls. The wet floor was strewn with trash.

Deputy Martin angled his flash so it illuminated the depths of the cave. A couple of bats scuttled away across the roof, squealing in protest at the intrusion.

"Nothing, Chief."

"Hold on." Deputy Morrison pointed his flash upward, toward the ceiling of the cave. The beam picked out the entrance to the secondary cavern. "I thought I remembered there was another cave in here."

Shugrue stared at him, and Morrison flushed. "We used to play in here when we were kids," he admitted. "Me and my brother."

"Then you'll know how to get up there," the sheriff stated. "Martin, keep your light trained on him."

Morrison crossed the floor and scrambled up. He cursed as his head broke through into the fouler air of the upper chamber.

"Nobody here, Chief," he called down. "Just a couple of candy wrappers, and—"

His voice trailed away. There was a moment's silence, then:

"And what, damn it?" Shugrue demanded in frustration.

In the smaller cavern, Deputy Morrison was frozen with fear and disgust. His hand trembled as he pointed his flashlight into the corner of the cave.

Lying there, matted in blood, its eyes frozen in a hideous stare, was a severed human head.

CHAPTER 13

Friday afternoon

"—station K-SAM, broadcasting from downtown Small-ville."

Martha sat at her kitchen table, cleaning and sorting the eggs, vegetables, and fruit Lex Luthor had ordered for his party. But her mind was only half on what she was doing. No matter how hard she tried, she couldn't forget what was happening to Clark.

She even found herself wondering if it was connected, somehow, to the death of Henry Tait and the attacks on the others.

"Breaking news this afternoon," the radio announcer went on, "is the naming of the suspect in the murder of Smallville High teacher Henry Tait. Sheriff Bryan Shugrue recently told this station the man he's looking for is Raymond Dansk, recently of the Metropolis Penitentiary. To tell us more, the sheriff has taken time off from his busy sched-ule—"

Martha carefully packed another carton of eggs and stacked it with the boxes piling up on the floor. Despite what Jonathan felt about him, Martha liked Lex Luthor. She believed he was an asset to the town. He'd already thrown a lifeline to several small farms like the Kents', buying up produce that might otherwise have been dumped.

He'd even offered to buy the Kent farm once—or "invest in it," as Lex had put it. Jonathan was outraged. Lex accepted the decision with his customary easy charm. "No sweat," he said. "It's only business."

But Lex was the Fertilizer King of Kansas—and Jonathan was fiercely organic. He allowed no chemicals on the farm. It meant their crops cost more to grow but sold for a higher price.

How could two such men ever see eye to eye?

She began packing a box of spring onions, her mind drifting back to the radio show.

"—one murder and two serious assaults in the past week," Bryan Shugrue was saying. "So far, we have only circumstantial evidence that Mr. Dansk is involved. It would be a big help to us, and eliminate him from our inquiries, if he could contact the Smallville sheriff's office."

"Crimes like these are commonplace in our big cities," the broadcaster's voice put in. "But for something of this nature to occur in an idyllic town like Smallville . . . any thoughts on that, Sheriff?"

Bryan Shugrue cleared his throat. "Smallville has had its fair share of mysteries and unsolved crimes in the past. This time, we know who we're looking for. Rest assured, we will find him."

Ray Dansk, Martha thought bleakly. Just one man, yet his actions—if indeed he were the murderer—were bringing fear and paranoia to a whole town. She thought of Jonathan, out in the fields with a search party, and prayed he would be all right.

"Weather news now. There's a serious storm headed our way. Weathergirl Heather is here to tell us all about it—"

Martha leaned across a stack of boxed mushrooms—grown in the farmhouse cellar—and switched off the radio. Jonathan had said a couple of days ago that storms were on the way. He'd spent a couple of hours earlier that morning battening down everything loose in the farmyard, making sure the animals were penned and fed and out of harm's way.

Murder—assault—the strange business with Clark and his powers—and now a storm. Country life was far from the stress-free idyll city folk supposed.

Jonathan walked slowly down the space between two rows of corn, swiveling his gaze from side to side.

He felt as if he were in another world. To either side of him the tall, thick cornstalks formed walls of green standing as high as his head. Shafts of sunlight played over them, disappearing as clouds passed in front of the sun.

Hope we find Dansk before the storm breaks.

A dozen of the local farmers had met up after lunch, their pickups and tractors and four-by-fours converging on a road junction a half mile outside the city limits. Nobody had much to say. They all knew why they were here, and what they had to do. If a murderer was hiding on their farms, or in their fields, it was their responsibility to find him.

Jonathan noticed a couple of them carrying shotguns. He wasn't a gun man himself, but he understood their caution. Ray Dansk—or his beast—had slain a grown man and nearly killed Peter Ross. It would be foolish to take risks with their own lives.

Others had brought their dogs, big, rangy mutts used to chasing rabbits and squirrels. But even they seemed to realize the seriousness of their task, and they strained at their leashes, eager for the hunt.

They lined up along the edge of a field, one man between each two rows. They moved off in unison, calling out occasionally to mark their progress to their companions.

Jonathan tried to stay alert, consciously forcing his eyes

to rove up and down the rows, seeking any unusual signs. The wind had whipped up some, and the cornstalks swayed and shook. If they didn't find Dansk before the storm hit, they wouldn't stand a chance in hell.

But his mind kept turning to Clark, and what was happening to the boy.

"I'm afraid you can't see him," the nurse said flatly. "He's in surgery."

Chloe, Lana, and Clark had just arrived in the bright, clean hospital reception area. All three had gone back to school at lunchtime, but the afternoon had been a disaster.

This was the day Henry Tait's essay should have been handed in. Out of the whole class, only Chloe had bothered to finish hers. He'd been her favorite teacher, and it was the only way she could think of to pay her final respects.

She'd hoped to spend the afternoon in the newspaper office, doing further research into the phantom beast phenomenon. But Principal Kwan himself decided to take their class, and she was forced to attend.

The principal had given a long, rambling speech in tribute to Mr. Tait, but instead of being cathartic, it only served to deepen the mood of gloom that hung over the class.

"Surgery?" Chloe repeated now. "But why? What's happened?"

The nurse flipped over a couple of sheets pinned to a clipboard. "Complications due to internal bleeding," she read out. "You're welcome to sit in the waiting room, but I'm afraid I have no idea how long it might be before we have any news."

"Is he going to be all right?" Lana demanded.

"I'm sure of it." The nurse sounded adamant, as if she'd brook no disagreement. "He's in good hands."

In silence, the trio trooped into the small waiting room. Pete's parents were already there, sitting close together, holding each other's hands.

"I'm so sorry," Clark told them. "If there's anything we can do—"

Mrs. Ross raised her tear-stained face. "Pray for him, Clark," she said quietly. "Just pray for him."

Pete Ross lay unconscious and unmoving on the operating table.

Pete knew that, because somehow he was floating near the ceiling, looking down on his own body and the team of surgeons and nurses gathered around it. To his disembodied consciousness, the operating theater seemed harshly bright and sterile. He didn't want to be there.

Instantly, he found himself drifting higher, passing right through the roof of the hospital as if he was a ghost. Looking down, he could see his parents in the waiting room, his mom sobbing, his dad comforting her with quiet words. His friend Clark sat between Chloe and Lana, holding each of their hands in his.

"There's no need to worry about me," Pete wanted to shout. "I'll be fine."

He tried to speak, but no sound came.

Ruefully, he wished he'd had the courage, just once, to ask Chloe to go out with him on a date. Not as friends. A date.

He was drifting higher now, and there was a tunnel of light in the sky above. A spiraling column of pure, white brilliance snaked away to infinity. It was the most beautiful thing Pete had ever seen.

He entered its mouth, and the light radiated into him from every angle. He started to move into the tunnel, his speed increasing as the light danced and glittered around him, shining more brightly with every passing moment. He thought he could see figures at the other end of the tunnel, where the light was so bright it was dazzling. They were waving and smiling, waiting for him.

Pete let himself be carried toward them, like a feather on the breeze. All of his woes and anxieties seemed to be seeping out of him, dissipating on contact with the magical light. They were baggage he no longer needed. Never again would he feel inadequate, unable to live up to the achievements and successes of his family.

Where he was going, it didn't matter if you were the runt of the litter.

He thought suddenly of his parents, and a wave of sadness swept through him. They'd always loved him as much as they loved his siblings. They'd always gone out of their way to impress on him that he was special, too. That success doesn't necessarily make you a better person. That everybody was unique.

They didn't deserve the grief his going would cause.

And his friends. They'd shared good times and bad times. They'd laughed and cried, been happy for each other, argued and cursed and vowed they'd never speak to each other again. They were at the start of their lives, and he belonged with them.

Maybe being Pete Ross wasn't so bad.

Suddenly, he found himself hurtling back down the tunnel of light, as if he'd been snapped back by a giant elastic band. The sparkling light faded around him, then he was plunging down through the cloudy sky, through the roof of the hospital, through the ceiling of the ward . . .

Toward himself.

A large rat balanced precariously on a floating log.

Whiskers twitching, it raised its snout in the air to sniff the gusting wind. Something had made it uneasy. Something was out of place.

The rat dipped, ready to plunge back into the water. The river meandered in a series of broad curves here, and floating garbage was often drawn into the bends by the crosscurrent. It became trapped there, rotating slowly, out of the main flow.

Suddenly, a hand broke the surface. The rat squealed, and tried to leap away, but it was too late. It was held fast, squirming and squeaking, vainly attempting to wriggle free.

Ray Dansk's head appeared from under the water beside the log. There was an inhuman look in his red-tinged eyes, and his lips drew back in a snarl as his feet scrabbled for purchase on the river bottom near the bank. He held the rat away from his face, uncaring as it bit the skin between his thumb and forefinger.

He gave a low growl and squeezed hard. The rat's struggles ceased, and its body went limp.

Dansk raised it to his mouth, and began to gnaw.

He hauled himself up onto the riverbank a few minutes later and sprawled full-length in the thick reeds that fringed it. He'd come fully five miles downstream, well clear of the city. They'd have to bring in choppers from the Big Met if they wanted to find him here.

The sun broke from behind a bank of dirty gray clouds. Dansk frowned as the light glinted on something in the grass. He rolled himself upright and went to investigate, squelching through the boggy ground.

It was a shard of a mirror, sticking out of the mud between rusty cans and plastic bottles. Carefully, he picked it up, and raised it to eye level.

It took him a minute to recognize the thing that stared back at him. Its wet hair was flat against its head. Its teeth were broken and chipped, and there were cuts around its mouth. Its eyes were sunken, and hollow, and red. Its skin was tinged with green.

It was himself.

Ray Dansk sank down in the reeds, laughing insanely.

"Doctor? How is he?"

Pete Ross senior leaped to his feet as the waiting room door opened and a white-coated doctor entered. He seemed taken aback to see so many people waiting for his pronouncement, as five faces stared expectantly at him.

Time seemed to stand still for all of them. Then the doctor spoke.

"I'm glad to say young Peter is doing well. He's going to make a full recovery."

There was a collective sigh of relief, then everyone was hugging everyone else, and Mrs. Ross's sobs changed to tears of joy.

CHAPTER 14

Friday evening

"I'm so glad Peter's on the mend," Martha said, ladling healthy portions of chicken and vegetables onto two plates. She passed them over to Jonathan and Clark, filled her own plate, and sat down at the dinner table.

"Great news, isn't it?" Clark savored the delicious aroma of the food. "Makes me feel like celebrating. I think I'll call Lana and treat her to the Beanery's finest."

"I'd rather you didn't, son," Jonathan said slowly. "We need to have a serious talk."

"I'm here, Dad."

"Let's eat first."

Jonathan and the other farmers had spent all afternoon combing the fields but had found no sign of Ray Dansk. By the time they called it a day, they must have searched several square miles of farmland and had nothing to show for their troubles except a liberal caking of dust.

Jonathan spent most of the time worrying about Clark and the dilemma his son's predicament was causing. Should they tell Clark more about his origins, in the hope it would spark his memory? Or should they leave things be, accept what was happening as the natural order of things, and wait to see what transpired?

They'd always been straight with the boy. There was no need for that to change now.

After dinner, Clark helped his father clear the table and heap the dishes on the drain board. Jonathan sat down again at the table, while Clark took an apple from the fruit bowl, polished it against his shirtsleeve, and sprawled into the cane chair by the range.

"I want you to listen, Clark, and not speak until I finish."

Crunch. Clark bit deep into the crisp fruit.

"Twelve years ago, a swarm of meteorites rained down on Smallville. Your mother and I found you wandering near a crater in the ground, out in the fields."

Crunch.

"In the crater, we found a small metallic spacecraft."

Cru—. Clark's teeth bit halfway into the apple, then froze.

"From the size of the craft, it was obvious that's where you'd come from."

"That's preposterous," Clark began, but Jonathan held up a hand to halt him.

"Hear me out, son. It didn't take long for us to discover you were different. Unique. You could pick up a fifty-pound sack of potatoes by the time you were six. You never had a bruise or cut, never suffered any childhood illness. As you got older, we found you could run faster than the tractor."

Jonathan's eyes never left his son's. The hand with the apple in it had fallen to Clark's side, and his mouth hung open as he tried to absorb what his father was saying.

"Mom?" Clark said weakly. "Are you going to hit me with the punch line?"

"The punch line is," Jonathan went on, "you're an alien. You don't come from this planet. But you've forgotten all about your past. Something's wrong."

Sudden anger flared in Clark's eyes. "There's something wrong, all right," he snapped, his voice bitter. He stood up, shoving back the chair so hard it toppled to the floor. "I know I'm nothing special, just a normal kid. But I thought that didn't matter. I thought you loved me anyway."

Unable to bear her son's anguish, Martha moved quickly to his side. Her arms wrapped him in a comforting hug.

"We do love you, Clark—more than anything. It's just— we're going crazy with worry, trying to figure out what's going on."

"Nothing's going on," Clark protested.

He gently disengaged himself from his mother's embrace and headed out through the porch into the yard.

"I'm going to the loft in the barn. I want to be alone."

Clouds dappled the moon, and the rising wind whipped through the trees in the old cemetery. The gravestones stood, mute and timeless, casting strange shadows in the intermittent moonlight. An owl hooted, and was answered by another, even closer by.

Good thing I'm used to this, Lana thought, turning up the collar of her jacket, *or I'd be totally spooked!*

She'd stayed at home for hours, hoping that Clark would call and arrange to meet her. But there was no word from him. She could have called him, of course, but she didn't want him to think she was being pushy. Falling in love with him had been so sudden, so unexpected, she no longer knew what normal social behavior should be.

Her Aunt Nell was back at the house with Deputy Martin. The officer had been assigned to stay overnight, in case Dansk or his beast showed up again. They'd have had a fit if they'd known Lana had sneaked out.

But she needed someone to talk to. And it was weeks since she'd visited her parents.

Their grave stood on a well-kept square of turf, surrounded by flowers she'd planted over the years. Her mother, Laura, had always loved flowers. Lana could remember their house always being full of a dozen fragrances, at all seasons.

Before the meteors fell.

The moon vanished behind a mass of black cloud, pitching the graveyard into total darkness. Lana heard a sound behind her. Startled, she turned.

It was only a plastic wreath, billowing against a plinth.

She sighed. This was the one place in the world where she truly felt safe. As if her parents were still watching her, from beyond the grave, still guiding her life. Still loving her.

She knelt before the simple marble headstone and bowed her head. The noise of the wind gusting in the branches seemed to fade.

"Hi, Mom. Dad. Sorry it's been so long since I visited."

She imagined she heard her mother's faint voice, telling her it was all right.

"I have a new boyfriend, Mom. I want to know what you think of Clark."

She listened intently for a moment, then smiled.

"Yes, I know he's neat, and clean, and handsome, and polite. Anybody could have told you that. But what do you *think* of him?"

Sometimes, she wondered if she was fooling herself. Was this just a charade played out in her own mind? Did her parents really speak to her, or did she just invent their words?

She saw them in her mind, not aged, but still the way they looked that fateful afternoon. Young, and strong, and full of hope for the future. Mom had dressed her as a fairy princess that morning, given her a sparkling magic wand. It was to be a magic day.

Then they went away and left her with Aunt Nell. She waved her wand and practiced her fairy spells until she was word-perfect.

Aunt Nell took her out to meet them. And the meteor fell, and the air was full of fire, and smoke, and screams.

And three-year-old Lana knew that her mommy and daddy were never coming back.

The ache still echoed in her heart.

She wished that magic wand was real, that it was in her hands now, so she could wave it in the way only fairies know and say the secret words that would heal her life and make her whole again.

Tears stung the back of her eyes, and she dashed them away with her knuckles.

She knew there was no going back.

Sadly, she got to her feet. Sometimes they spoke to her, sometimes they didn't. It didn't mean they weren't there, watching. It didn't mean they didn't love her.

Suddenly, a howl of wind blew a passage in the clouds. The moon emerged in all its glory, flooding the graveyard in pale silvery light.

"Clark is a fine young man, but he's not the man for you. Not now, Lana."

Did her mother really say that? Did she just imagine it? It certainly wasn't what she'd wanted to hear.

But it didn't change her feelings any.

The gap in the clouds was short-lived, and again they piled up on each other, as if competing to see which would claim the honor of smothering the remaining moonlight.

Her heart heavier than when she climbed up, Lana set out down the hill.

Somewhere close, a frog was croaking.

Ray Dansk lay in the reed bed, oblivious to the marsh water that soaked him to the skin. He'd never really listened to a frog before. Now he could hear every nuance in its voice. Whatever it was saying, it had a certain poetry.

In the sky above, the moon bobbed through the clouds like a buoy on the ocean.

For the first time since he could remember, he felt at peace with himself. At one. Everything was preordained. Events had been set in motion. Consequences would follow. All Ray Dansk had to do was show up and play his part.

He closed his eyes, and dreamed of blood.

The barn smelled of old wood and straw.

Clark sat with his back against the slatted wall. Anger and dismay, resentment and incomprehension all churned inside him. An alien? His parents must be crazy!

Trying to calm himself, he swiveled his telescope to the east, where the sky was still clear. Gazing unblinkingly through the eyepiece, he could make out a faint smudge in an otherwise blank patch of sky. Another galaxy, he knew, one among so many millions that astronomers gave them numbers instead of names.

And the galaxies were grouped in clusters, millions of them, each containing trillions of stars. And the clusters themselves were part of unbelievably massive superclusters, in a process that might repeat itself for all eternity. Like fractals of fractals of fractals.

What was it Henry Tait had told his class? "We're all responsible for ourselves." Maybe that's the only way a universe of increasing complexity could run itself. If every part was responsible for itself.

Could it be true? Could I really come from out there, from some planet light-years away, an unobserved dot lost in the vastness of space?

Angrily, he brushed the thought away. The whole idea was ridiculous. Insane!

So what was it with his mother and father? Why had they concocted this elaborate fantasy? Was it some kind of double delusion, each feeding off the other's madness? How could two normal adults deteriorate into such wild flights of fancy, and keep up the pretense no matter what?

Why are they doing it? A sudden thought struck him with unexpected ferocity. *Or . . . is it me that's going insane? Because that's how I'm starting to feel!*

Outside, the massing clouds swept down on the moon. Already, in the far distance, sheet lightning cracked and branched; celestial spider webs, illumining the clouds like electric hell.

Blotting out his own racing thoughts, Clark swung the telescope toward the storm. He stopped as the barrel aligned with Lana's house. He let it linger there, taking in the closed curtains with light seeping out around the edges. There was a deputy's car parked outside.

He hadn't called her, he remembered suddenly. And it was way too late now.

Incongruously, he found himself wondering what Lana would say if he told her he was an alien. He imagined consternation on her pretty face and almost laughed out loud at the thought. His grim mood lifted a little.

He was a normal guy, with a normal life. The only thing abnormal about him was his luck—for wasn't he taking the prettiest girl in the world to the party tomorrow night?

Then he thought of his parents again, and his mind plunged back into a maelstrom.

He slipped the protective cover over the lens, and covered the telescope away for the night. He made his way over to the ladder and quickly descended to the barn below.

As he closed the barn doors behind him, heavy black clouds flooded over the moon like a tidal wave.

"Dad? It's me. Lex."

Lex stood on the battlements of his castle, glorying in the coming storm. The Stars and Stripes that flew above was blowing horizontal, snapping like a bullwhip in the wind.

He pressed his cell phone to his ear and imagined his father's irritation. He smiled.

"Lex? What the hell are you playing at? Don't you know it's 4 A.M. in Dublin?"

"Yes."

"Don't you know *I'm* in Dublin?"

"Yes."

"Then what the hell are you doing waking me up like this?"

"I'm calling to say thanks for your offer, Dad—but no thanks."

"What? What are you talking about? You'd better have a damned good explanation for this, boy."

"Renata."

There was a pause that told Lex all he wanted to know. He knew he had struck the nerve he was aiming for.

"I don't know what you're talking about, Lex."

"You don't know when to stop lying, Dad," Lex replied flatly. "Renata didn't come up with that crazy story on her own. Someone put her up to it. How much did you pay her?"

"Fifty K," Lionel Luthor said defensively. "If you'd given her the million, she was to keep it."

"Why, Dad? Was it some kind of test of my morality? Did you want to know if I'd play with dirty money? Or was it just because you can't stop interfering in my life?"

Silence.

"Why, Dad?"

Pause. "Why not, Lex?"

Click.

Lex glared at his cell phone as the call disengaged. He shook his head in disbelief that quickly turned to some kind of warped admiration. His father had wriggled off the hook . . . again.

He'd probably never know why Lionel had done it. It could have been any of the reasons Lex had suggested. Or, like the purchase of the Scottish castle, maybe he'd just done it because he could.

Lex closed his eyes and raised his face to the wind.

CHAPTER 15

Saturday morning

The wind dropped sometime during the night, and it started to rain, a light but steady drizzle that soaked through everything it touched. The dry ground absorbed the water greedily.

There was no discernible sunrise, merely clouds turning a lighter shade of gray.

Lying in the marsh where he'd stayed all night, wet through to the bone, Ray Dansk didn't shiver in the dawn chill. He was feasting on some inner warmth, the fiery flames of his hatred.

In a strange way, he felt at home here. Dragons lived in swamps, don't they? Or is it caves?

Who cared?

For the third time since rising, Lana filled the three mugs with steaming coffee.

Deputy Martin had stayed outside all night, at first patrolling the garden with his flashlight and drawn gun. But when the rain began, depressing and persistent, he retired to his car. He sat in the passenger seat with his gun on his knee, fighting to stave off the desire for sleep.

Lana had gone out to fetch him in the cold morning rain and found him stretching his legs in the yard, stiff and aching from his lonely vigil.

They breakfasted on pancakes and maple syrup, listening to the news on the radio. A serial killer had been arrested in Metropolis, and five members of the same family were killed by a drunk driver close to the state line. But there was no mention of the Smallville Beast.

Lana was disappointed that Clark hadn't called last night, but she knew he must have his reasons. She intended to spend the whole day getting ready for the party—an idea that was soon scotched by Deputy Martin.

"Your aunt wants to spend the day in town," he explained. "I can't leave you here alone—and I can't be in two places at once. So," he concluded, "you have to come to town, too."

"Please, Aunt Nell," Lana pleaded. "You know how important tonight is."

But Nell Potter was firmly on the deputy's side. "Leave you here on your own? What if that thing came back? No, Lana—you're coming with me. And we'll stay in the hotel tonight. We're not coming back here until the damage is repaired."

Scowling, Lana went upstairs to pack what she would need in a travel bag.

The rain was by no means heavy, but it was persistent enough for slickers and rubber boots.

"So where are we going?" Clark asked, trudging away from the farm behind his father. "What's the big mystery?"

Please, he was praying, *don't let it be anything like last night! I don't think I got a wink of sleep, for worrying about you and Mom. I'm not able to take any more weirdness!*

"You'll see," Jonathan told him enigmatically.

Walking briskly, Jonathan turned off the track, taking a little-used path that ran alongside a field.

He and Martha had talked long into the night, discussing all the options that were open to them. It boiled down to two choices: Do nothing, or try to shock Clark into remembering the truth.

After much discussion and dissent, they'd finally agreed on the latter.

"Nearly there now," Jonathan grunted, stepping onto the grassy banking to avoid a patch of deep mud.

In a few more minutes father and son were standing beside a small group of willow trees. Rain dripped from their leaves, pooling on the ground. A dense curtain of underbrush grew beneath the trees, obscuring any view of what the little grove contained.

Clark followed as Jonathan skirted the bushes. In the middle of them, virtually invisible until they were right on top of it, was a low storm cellar.

Jonathan pulled a key from the pocket of his raincoat and jammed it into the large padlock that held the low, wooden door closed. He hardly ever came out here, and it took a lot of turning and twiddling before the key would turn in the rusting lock.

It gave at last, and Jonathan barged the heavy door open with his shoulder. He beckoned to Clark to follow him and stooped under the low doorframe.

It was almost pitch-dark inside. The air smelled slightly musty, and there was a faint odor of something unusual, almost like sulfur. Jonathan unclipped his flashlight from his belt and snapped on the beam.

The interior was a mess. Wooden beams and fence posts and plastic sheeting lay awry on the sunken floor. A roll of fencing wire, partly unraveled, snaked across the debris. It was as if the place had been filled with junk, then abandoned.

Jonathan felt Clark's puzzled gaze bore into him as, carefully, he stooped to move aside a couple of the heavy beams. He rolled back a sheet of blue farm plastic and tugged away the tarpaulin beneath it.

He stood back, giving Clark plenty of space to see what was hidden there.

Picked out in the flashlight's bright glare was a small metallic object, not much larger than a wide-screen television. From its shape, there could be no doubt what it was.

A tiny spacecraft.

"Yay! Rebel's got a scent!"

The powerful German shepherd dog exited from the cave, its leash taut as it pulled Deputy Morrison along behind it.

"He's definitely onto something," Morrison continued, as the dog snuffled at the wet ground. He whined quietly, and tried to pull Morrison away.

"Good. Any trail won't last long in this." Sheriff Shugrue nodded his satisfaction. Dressed in slickers and rubber boots, he looked as if he'd put on another twenty pounds.

Preliminary forensic results on Henry Tait's body had come in by fax the previous night. There was a lot of technical stuff, about the nature of the wounds, their depth, and the integrity of the wound edges. What it came down to was what Shugrue had originally maintained: attack by animal, or animals, unknown.

Shugrue had had the tracker dog brought in from Otsville, sixty miles to the east and twice the size of Smallville. Its handler was in Las Vegas on vacation, but Shugrue talked his Otsville counterpart into sending the dog over anyhow.

This Ray Dansk was running rings around him, and Shugrue didn't like it. Whatever beast he was using to make the attacks, it had to be stopped before there was another death. And the fact that Dansk had taken Tait's head . . . the man was obviously psychotic. The sooner he was back behind bars, the better Shugrue would like it.

"Give him his head," he told Morrison.

The deputy eased the pressure on the leash, and Rebel moved away from the cave entrance, muzzle to the ground. Shugrue and Deputy Ryan followed.

The dog took an indirect route, heading toward the river, weaving from bush to bush and tree trunk to clump of long grass.

"Looks like the creep was real careful about his getaway," Morrison remarked. "He wasn't taking any chances on being seen."

Finally, the dog stopped at the riverbank, turning its head first this way, then that. It started to whine, looking up at Shugrue as if somehow it blamed him for the scent's disappearance.

"He must have taken to the water," Shugrue decided. "Walk the dog upstream until you find where he came out."

"What if he went downstream, Sheriff? Or came out on the far bank?"

"Check them and see," Shugrue ordered. "A couple of miles in each direction."

Grumbling to himself at the mammoth task ahead, Morrison set off upstream with the dog.

The sheriff turned to Ryan. "Any word from Martin?"

"Yes, sir. He escorted Miss Potter and her niece into town. He says he'll stay with them until he hears from you."

"And Deputy Walker's still at the Luthor Mansion?"

Ryan nodded, and Shugrue began to walk away. "I'm going over there. You'd better go help Morrison."

"Don't you want to know why I did it?"

Renata and Lex were in bed in Lex's turret room, sprawled on royal blue silk sheets, enjoying the late breakfast Louis Verne—accompanied by his shadow, Deputy Walker—had brought them. She watched Lex intently, concerned that, after his phone call to his father, he hadn't said another word to her about the matter.

Lex shrugged as he raised a triangle of toast and marmalade to his mouth. "Money. To get back at me for some reason. Objectively, it doesn't matter."

"What do you mean?"

Lex finished chewing before he answered. "What we think doesn't matter. What we feel doesn't matter. The only thing that's important is what we *do*. Our behavior."

Renata felt uncomfortable at his words. It wasn't as if she didn't feel guilty enough already. She'd taken Lionel Luthor's money to pull a scam on his son, a man she'd once loved. She had no idea why Lionel wanted it done, only that he'd paid her fifty thousand dollars, which she badly needed.

"I know what you're like," Lex went on. "I wouldn't have been true to myself if I hadn't suspected you."

Not liking where the conversation was going, Renata changed the subject. "Why did your father do it?"

"You're not listening, Renata." Lex sighed and reached for his coffee cup. "It doesn't matter why he did it. It only matters that he did it."

Renata screwed up her face, trying to make sense of his

philosophy. She failed. "Do you want me to leave?" she asked in a small voice.

"No hurry," Lex said expansively. "Stay for the party."

Deputy Martin bit into his donut, turned to the next page of the comic book, and thanked his lucky stars.

He was sitting on a thoughtfully provided chair in Smallville's largest department store, whiling away the time as Nell Potter did her shopping. "Stay with them," Sheriff Shugrue had ordered—and that's exactly what he was doing.

Fleetingly, he thought of Morrison and the others, combing the riverbank in the mud and rain. Sometimes it wasn't so bad being a cop. Why, Walker even got to stay at the Luthor Castle.

Deputy Martin smiled, took another bite, and flicked to the next page.

"Aunt Nell—I have to go home—right now!"

Lana's face was a picture of distress. She'd been rummaging in her bag and suddenly realized she'd left something behind. Clark's tiepin.

"I thought we settled that, Lana. I'm here, you're here, the deputy's here." She gestured to the shelves and displays around her. "And we're staying here until I find replacements for everything that was smashed the other night."

"You don't understand," Lana complained. "I forgot Clark's gift. I left it behind when you hurried me out this morning. I'm supposed to be giving it to him at the party tonight."

"It'll just have to wait. We won't be going back to the house until the glazier has replaced the broken windows. I've already reserved rooms at the hotel for tonight."

Nell turned back to the display of photo frames she'd been studying.

Lana sighed. She'd been looking forward to the party. She had no intention of spoiling things now.

"I'm going to the rest room," she said, and stalked off.

The rest room doors were hidden from Aunt Nell and the deputy's view by a row of hardware displays. Lana walked right past them and instead pushed open the door to the stairwell. She took a last look to make sure she hadn't been seen, then hurried downstairs.

Minutes later, Lana was a block away, hailing a yellow cab cruising down the street. Tonight was important. She wanted everything to be perfect.

The cab pulled up beside her, and she slipped into the rear seat.

"The Potter place, please."

Clark stared at the miniature spacecraft in total disbelief.

"One end of it was damaged by the impact," his father was saying. "But there's no denying what it is. It was obviously made for a child, too, because no adult would fit in it. I can't find any means of propulsion, and I don't have a clue as to how to open it up."

Clark was like a statue. Paralyzed. His mind refused to function. This was so far outside all his normal frames of reference, he just couldn't take it in.

"While Martha took care of you, I used the tractor to drag the ship here. We didn't want anyone else finding it, in case they guessed the truth about you."

Clark looked blankly at him.

"If the authorities found out there was an alien child here," Jonathan explained gently, "they'd have taken you away from us. And your mother—well, she thought you were the answer to our prayers. I couldn't bear to see her heart broken."

Clark stood in stunned silence, trying to assimilate everything his father had said.

"This can't be true," he burst out at last. "I don't know why you're doing this to me, but it's not a joke anymore, Dad!"

"It never was a joke, son. It's deadly serious."

"Stop it! Stop it!"

He turned away from the light and barged out of the building, banging his head against the low door lintel.

"Clark!" Jonathan called after him. "Come back!"

But Clark was already running into the fields. The wind snatched at his clothes, and the rivulets of rain that ran down his face felt like tears.

"You can't do this, Sheriff. It's inhumane!"

Lex Luthor held up his hands, palms out, in protest. But Bryan Shugrue's grim look told him the cop was adamant.

"I'm sorry, Mr. Luthor," the sheriff said, "but I need Deputy Walker for the manhunt. Stands to reason Dansk could make another attempt on Verne's life—so I'd rather have him downtown, where the deputies can keep an eye on him."

Louis Verne came out to join them on the front steps of the castle. The overhanging stone porch protected them from the rain that dripped steadily over its edges.

"But Louis is tonight's star," Lex tried again. "And he'll be safe enough here. I've hired a couple of security guards."

The sheriff shook his head. He motioned to Louis to follow him, then hurried through the rain to his car, parked on the gravel. Deputy Walker was already seated inside.

"But I need him to cook for 120 people!" Lex shouted.

"Sorry, Mr. Luthor," Shugrue called back. "Looks like you'll have to get takeout!"

Lex closed the heavy door as the sheriff's car sped off in a spray of gravel chips. Of course, it was more important that Louis was safe in protective custody than to have him at the castle, where he could more easily be exposed to danger.

Lex chewed his lip, deep in thought. Who the hell was going to do the cooking?

Renata?

He threw back his head and laughed.

Lana switched on her bedroom light, and gave a little shudder.

The window broken by the intruder had been boarded up, shutting out the natural light, and the broken glass was all cleared up. But Lana could still feel his presence, as if he'd left some part of himself behind.

Shaking off her morbid thoughts, she bent to rummage in the jewelry drawer of her makeup cabinet. Her fingers closed around the silver star tiepin, and she pulled it out with a smile.

She switched off the light and hurried downstairs. Outside the front door, the cab was sitting waiting, its engine still running. With a little luck, she'd be able to make it back to the store before anybody missed her. The deputy had been engrossed in his comic books, and Nell became oblivious to all else when she was shopping.

But as she grasped the cab door handle, she saw a figure stumbling out from the corn beyond the garden fence.

Lana's heart skipped a beat, as she remembered the horror of her aunt being attacked.

But this was no beast.

It was Clark.

She ran across the sodden grass to meet him, heedless of the rain against the hair she'd spent an hour brushing.

He looked miserable. His hair stuck to his head, curly wisps dripping a miniature rain down his face. His clothes were soaked through, and he was covered up to the ankles in mud. He was obviously very upset. Lana didn't hesitate. Yelling to the cabby to wait a little longer, please, she helped Clark up the steps to the front door.

Moments later, they were inside.

"You get out of those wet clothes before you catch your death of cold," Lana ordered. "You can take a shower while I dry them off."

She watched anxiously as Clark climbed the stairs to the bathroom.

"Mrs. Kent?"

"Clark's not home right now." Martha recognized the voice on the other end of the telephone line. "Can I take a message for him?"

She'd finished packing the food half an hour earlier, and had spent the time since fretting about what Jonathan and Clark were doing.

"It wasn't Clark I wanted, Mrs. Kent," she heard Lex Luthor say. "It's you. My chef, Louis, has been taken into protective custody by the police, leaving me high and dry. I'm not exactly Chef Boyardee."

There was a short pause, and just as Martha was about to ask why he was telling her this, Lex told her.

"Clark's always boasting about your cooking. I was wondering . . . would you be available today? Right away, in fact?"

CHAPTER 16

Saturday afternoon

Clark had showered and dried. Now he sat in the lounge, feeling faintly ridiculous wearing Nell Potter's dressing gown. Lana knelt on the rug at his side, as he stared morosely into the ashes of the dead fire.

"What's happened to upset you like this, Clark?" she asked in concern. "Has something happened to your parents?"

"No." Clark paused, then shrugged ruefully. "Well, yes. Something *has* happened to my parents. Something so weird, Chloe wouldn't even put it on her wall at the *Torch* office."

The floodgates opened, and all the concern he'd been bottling up inside came pouring out in one massive surge. "They seem to have gone crazy. They've been trying to tell me I'm abnormal," he went on scathingly. "An alien! Like, I have these fantastic powers—I can leap over buildings, and bench-press a tractor. I mean, is it normal to say things like that to your son? Is it some kind of phase parents go through, and nobody told me?"

His shoulders slumped again, and Lana squeezed them as hard as she could. "I've never heard anything like it. I guess all adults do weird stuff, but what you're talking about is taking it to the edge. You know," she added thoughtfully, "maybe they're trying to motivate you. Make you stronger by believing you're stronger."

"Sure," Clark scoffed, "motivate your son by telling him he's a space cadet. A very successful gambit."

"Don't be mad at me, Clark," Lana said quietly.

Clark was immediately contrite. "I'm sorry. I really didn't mean to take it out on you," he said hastily. He moved her arm and shifted his own till it arced around her shoulders, drawing her close to him. "The last thing in the world I'd want is to hurt you."

Lana tilted her head closer to his, and Clark closed his eyes, drinking in her nearness. She smelled wonderful.

When his eyes blinked open, her mouth was only inches away.

Clark moved, and their lips met gently. He felt an electric tingle shoot through his nervous system. His heart began pounding so hard, he was sure she'd hear it.

Lana moaned softly, and he drew her even closer, feeling her warmth against him. The kiss grew more urgent, more insistent, deep and long and full of the love they felt for each other.

Clark's temples throbbed, and his blood sang in his veins as, at last, he drew reluctantly away.

"I hope you have plenty of cash on you," he joked. "There's a cab waiting outside."

Lana yelped. "Yipes. We've been ages. Aunt Nell will flay me alive!"

Clark grabbed his clothes, and hurried upstairs to change.

"I've searched everywhere, Martha."

Jonathan peeled off his slickers in the porch, water dripping from them to puddle on the floor.

"He's not down at the pond, or in the meadow, or in his den in the barn. I just don't know where else to look."

His wife handed him a towel, and he began to dry his hair and face.

"I guess telling him was the wrong thing to do. He looked totally stunned. I should never have—"

"It's not your fault, Jonathan. We made the decision together."

"I know, but—"

"Everything's easy with hindsight," Martha reminded him. "Isn't that what you used to tell me? We did what we thought was right. That's what matters. Clark will come home when he's good and ready."

She gestured at the kitchen floor, piled high with boxes and cartons of fruit and vegetables. "It couldn't happen at a worse time. I've promised Lex Luthor I'll do the catering for the party tonight. I was just about to load this in the car when you showed up."

"Cooking for Luthor?" Jonathan looked horrified. "At a time like this? Our son needs us, Martha."

"Our son is a guest at this party, Jonathan Kent. I thought this would be a good way of keeping an eye on him. If he exhibits any more strange behavior, at least I'll be right on hand to deal with it."

"If he shows up," Jonathan said doubtfully.

"Lex is his best friend. And Clark bought a gift for Lana. Believe me, he'll be there."

They heard a car horn honking out in the yard. Martha hurried to open the door. Clark was waving to Lana as her cab turned to leave the farm again. Head down, he sprinted across the yard through the rain.

"Clark, where have you been?" Martha asked, as he squeezed past her into the kitchen.

"Lana's," he told her curtly. "We're meeting up later, at the party. That is—if aliens are allowed to go to parties."

He stalked off to his room, leaving Jonathan and Martha exchanging uncomfortable glances. How were they going to put *this* right?

"You're lucky, young lady. Real lucky."

Deputy Martin glowered angrily at Lana. She stood shamefaced, having just been caught trying to sneak in through the department store's fire exit.

"I was just about to put out a bulletin on you. You scared your aunt half-witless."

"I'm sorry, Aunt Nell," Lana apologized. "I just wanted Clark's gift, and that was the only way to get it. And the cab driver was there the whole time," she added hurriedly, "so I wasn't really in any danger."

Nell considered her niece. "I suppose there's no harm done," she said grudgingly. Then her eyes twinkled. "But for the rest of the afternoon, I'm handcuffing you to the deputy!"

"I don't get it, Lex," Renata said. "Why are you hosting a party for kids, anyway?"

Lex waved her away and turned his back. He was speaking into his cell phone, ensuring that the band he'd booked weren't drunk and incapable in a Metropolis hotel room. He'd even sent his own limousine to pick them up.

Renata studied his back thoughtfully. It intrigued her that he should want to mix with kids. It couldn't be because he wanted to regain his lost youth. Lex had led a wild life, but he'd turned his back on it. Like he said: "I grew up."

Maybe he wanted to ingratiate himself with the locals. But that wasn't the Lex she knew, either. He didn't know what "ingratiate" meant.

He flipped off his cell phone and turned back to her.

"What were you saying?"

"I was asking you—why a party for kids?"

Lex looked at her for a moment, then his face split in a wide grin. "As a wise man once said"—he shrugged expressively—"why not?"

"Good to see you, man," Pete said weakly.

The respirator had been removed, and he was sitting up in bed. He was still pale, and he'd spent most of the day sleeping, but Clark was just glad he was going to be okay.

At Clark's taciturn request, his father had driven him to the hospital. Neither spoke a word on the entire journey. After a short chat with Pete, Jonathan had gone off to find a coffee machine, leaving Clark alone with his friend.

"You were really brave the other night. You saved Nell Potter's life."

"Aw, shucks," Pete said modestly. "You'd have done the same thing—if you hadn't been stone-cold kayoed."

"Yeah? Anyway, I just want you to know I'm proud of you, Pete."

"That's what my dad said, too." He gave a wan smile. "Maybe I should get myself slashed by a phantom beast more often. Great way to gain status."

They sat talking for a while longer. Chloe had come to visit him earlier in the day, bringing fruit and books—and a copy of the paper she'd written for Henry Tait.

"Cool, huh?" Pete waved the pages at Clark. "I might be the only guy who ever reads it."

The nurse came in to announce it was time for Pete's bed bath. He groaned as Clark got to his feet.

"Think of me, dude," he said wistfully, "when you party tonight. Believe me, I'll be with you in spirit!"

Lightning split the air in an explosion of blue-white streaks. Seconds later, thunder roared and rumbled across the Kansas flatlands.

Ray Dansk felt the first fat drops of rain—real rain—splatter against his head. He held his mouth wide open, leaning back, drinking in the heavy droplets. But it wasn't the same as the cave water.

This was only rain.

Grinning like some predator contemplating its next bloody meal, he struck out through the marsh toward solid ground.

It was time for the Dragon to party.

CHAPTER 17

Saturday night

Jonathan steered the four-by-four through sheets of rain, up the drive toward the castle.

Sitting in the passenger seat, Clark could barely make out the trees through the downpour. The castle itself was all but invisible, despite the new security lighting Lex had installed since the night of the assault.

A massive bolt of lightning jagged suddenly across the sky, lighting up the castle in stark, electric relief.

"Impressive." Jonathan tried to sound conversational. "That's how it must have looked back in its native Scotland. I gather they get a lot of storms and rain there."

Clark murmured in agreement. His mother had left for Lex's hours earlier. Apart from the visit to Pete, he and his father had been alone together all that time. And not another word about spacecraft and aliens had been mentioned. He knew his father was afraid that saying the wrong thing might lead to a serious argument.

Clark *wanted* to argue, to thrash the whole business out until it made sense to him. But it would wait until tomorrow. He was determined nothing would spoil tonight.

The driveway widened dramatically as it curved around the castle, and dozens of cars and pickup trucks were already parked. Jonathan braked to a halt as close as he could get to the gatehouse and turned to Clark.

"You're going to need this," his father said, holding out a

black, furled umbrella. "Unless hair gel is more impervious to rain than it was in my day."

Clark forced himself to smile and took the umbrella from his father's hand. He was wearing his best suit—not exactly designer gear, but it fit well—and didn't want to get soaked.

"Thanks," he muttered ungraciously, as he unlocked the catch on his door.

"You make sure you have fun. And if you bump into your mother, try not to get roped into kitchen duty."

Despite himself, Clark smiled for real. He'd never quarreled as seriously as this with his parents before, and he didn't like how it was making him feel. "I'll avoid her like the plague."

He was just about to push the car door open when Jonathan leaned across and gripped his arm. "You're only young once, son. Your mother and I want you to enjoy it while you can."

"I will, Dad."

He opened the car door and slid out, unfurling the umbrella and angling it against the driving rain.

Then he bent his head and raced for the gatehouse entrance, the wind whipping around him.

Martha had almost panicked when Lex first showed her into the massive castle kitchens. Food of all descriptions was stacked everywhere, freezers and refrigerators groaning under the weight of the burgers and salads they contained. Hundreds of glasses, only half of them unpacked from their cardboard cartons, covered the work surfaces. Sacks of potatoes and onions were propped against a wall.

As her gaze roved over the huge room, wondering where on earth she was going to start, Lex handed her a sheet of paper with handwriting on it.

"Louis claimed the secret of a good burger was in the relish," he told her. "So I had him write down his favorite recipes, in case you want to try them."

"When will I have time?" Martha asked. "There's more than enough for one person to do as it is."

"I have two waitresses coming in later," Lex replied. "Besides, you don't have to do it alone. Help is at hand."

Puzzled, Martha looked around. There was nobody else there. Then she remembered—Clark had mentioned he had a girlfriend staying with him.

"Your girlfriend?"

"Fat chance."

It was only when she saw Lex roll back the sleeves of his black silk shirt that she understood what he meant.

"Ready when you are, maestro." He grinned, and Martha couldn't help but be won over by his boyish charm and enthusiasm. "Your wish is my command."

Martha fastened her apron around her waist, grinning to herself in anticipation of seeing Lex Luthor chopping onions and peeling potatoes.

Eventually, Lex's kitchen duties were over, and he had snapped into host mode.

His fine cotton jacket rustled gently as he took Clark's arm and guided him toward the great hall. Many of the antiques in the hallways had been discreetly moved to more secure locations, but the larger ones still occupied their permanent positions. They passed under the Byzantium lead crucifix, and went through the carved doorway beyond.

As they entered the huge, vaulted hall, a waitress stepped forward and handed each of them a glass of non-alcoholic fruit punch. Clark recognized her—she often worked in the Beanery on weekends.

"Mrs. Kent's special recipe," the girl informed them.

"I know it well," Clark responded. "Best in town."

He and Lex clinked glasses in a wordless toast and sipped their punch.

Renata came over to join them, mesmerizing in a silk dress that clung to her curves and flashed her thigh with every step.

"Hi, Clark," she said, reaching to airkiss his cheek.

He was surprised she remembered his name—unless, of course, Lex had briefed her. She slipped an arm around Lex's waist and began to nuzzle on his ear.

Clark took the opportunity to look around, drinking in the party. Light from the chandeliers reflected off the huge stained-glass window Lionel Luthor had installed.

A rock band had set up their equipment on the minstrel's gallery, and the long-haired singer's head swung to and fro as he intoned the lyrics to a heavy metal anthem. "The Mushrooms," they were called.

Clark had heard some of the cooler kids at school talking about them. Pete, who was always one jump ahead of everybody else in finding new bands, raved about them. They had a strong cult following, exactly the type of band who'd impress your friends when you said you saw them live, before they made it big and sold out to the stadium circuit.

Dozens of people were on the dance floor, bathed in multicolored strobe lights, looking like extras in a sixties psychedelic movie. Dozens more stood around the hall, or sat on the antique oak benches, eating and drinking and talking.

"You know how to throw a party," Clark told his friend admiringly.

"And how to invite the right guests."

Clark followed Lex's gesture and saw Lana for the first time. She was chatting to Marian Flitch, a senior at school. Her lithe body swayed slightly in synch with the heavy beat.

He'd always thought Lana the prettiest girl he'd ever seen, but he wasn't prepared for this. She wore a simple black dress cut low at the bodice and high at the knee. Her dark hair was piled on top of her head, like a Regency beauty. *And that's what she is,* Clark marveled. *Beautiful. Perfect.*

She turned her head and caught his gaze, and for the first time Clark understood the old cliché about eyes meeting across a crowded room. The pounding music and chattering voices seemed to fade to a murmur. The dancers and everybody else blurred into the background.

There was only him and Lana in the whole wide world.

"Excuse me, Lex," he muttered. He put his drink down on a table and began to walk toward her.

They met halfway across the dance floor. In silence, they took each other's hands. Their lips brushed lightly.

Then, still without saying a word, they began to dance.

Whitney Fordman stepped back into the stone-lined alcove, feeling like he'd been kicked in the heart.

He knew Lana and Kent would be here tonight. He knew he would feel jealous seeing them together. But he hadn't prepared himself for anything like this.

Lana looked sexier than he'd ever seen her. She was a great dancer, her body moving hypnotically in time to the music.

And yet it was Kent she was staring at, enrapt. It was Kent whose hand she was holding. It was Kent who—

"What's with the big brood, Whitney?" Rod Gaynor, another football player, asked. "It's a party, man. Chill."

"Thanks for your concern, Rod, but I'm okay," Whitney responded, his surly voice belying his words.

Rod smelled his breath. "Tell me you haven't been drinking, Whit."

"I had a couple of beers. So what? What do you care?"

"You're on a downward slide, dude." Rod shrugged and

moved away to head off the cute waitress with the drinks tray.

Whitney leaned back against the rough stone wall, breathing deeply, wrestling with the green-eyed monster that was playing havoc with his emotions.

What does that geek have that I don't? It makes me sick to watch them!

He stood there, unmoving, and his fierce glare never left them.

Nobody about. No surprise. You'd have to be crazy to be out on a night like this.

Ray Dansk didn't see the irony in his thoughts as he moved stealthily along the hedgerow, out of sight of the road. He was making for the neon lights of the motel/diner he could see through the rain a few hundred yards ahead.

Soaked, muddy, and bedraggled, he gloried in the raindrops that burst against him.

Above, the night was a broiling mass of dark thunderheads. Every few minutes, lightning tore holes in the sky.

He emerged from the end of the hawthorn hedge, directly opposite the diner. Through the rain-curtained windows, he could make out the blurred shapes of a couple of customers. There was only one vehicle in the parking lot, a chopped-down Harley Davidson motorbike. No doubt it was the riders he could see inside, sheltering from the storm.

Blinking the rain from his eyes, Dansk stole over to the bike. No keys were in the ignition, but that presented no problem to someone who knew as much about bikes as Dansk did. His fingers probed under the ignition casing and pulled out the wires.

Less than ten seconds later, he was astride the 1,000cc

monster, throttling hard. The chrome exhaust wailed as the big bike fishtailed down the road.

He was going to arrive at the party in style.

"I thought I wasn't going to get in," Lana said. "I couldn't find my invitation anywhere. I must have left it at home when Aunt Nell hustled me out."

She and Clark were standing underneath a large medieval tapestry that depicted hunting scenes in fourteenth-century Italy. His arm was around her waist, and he loved the way she rested her head lightly against his chest.

"Don't tell me," Clark guessed. "Lex took personal charge?"

Lana nodded. "A lot of people don't seem to like him. But I think he's charming."

And charismatic, and good-looking, and rich, Clark thought, with the faintest twinge of jealousy. He caught himself. *Jealous of my best friend? Crazy!*

There was a squeal from some girls standing nearby, and they turned toward the commotion. Lex's conjuror, dressed in robes and pointed hat like Gandalf the Gray, had just produced a handful of cell phones, seemingly from thin air. He handed them to the girls, and with a swirl of his colorful cloak spun around to face Lana and Clark. "Romeo and Juliet," he declared theatrically. "How may the powers of magic help fulfill your deepest desires?"

Lana flushed, and Clark reddened, too.

"I think we're happy enough with each other, thanks," he said, and Lana squeezed his arm.

The conjuror touched a finger to the peak of his hat, and the air filled instantly with a scattering of silver glitter.

Lana laughed, and Clark closed his eyes, savoring the moment.

"How come such a pretty girl is standing on her own?"

Chloe started in surprise as Lex Luthor spoke softly in her ear. She hadn't heard him come up behind her. *Too engrossed in Clark and Lana,* she thought, and sighed aloud. *I'd die to have Clark look at me like that.*

But Chloe Sullivan wasn't the type to fade away and waste time pining for any man. She loved life too much for that. Sure, it would be nice if she and Clark could get together. But it seemed they couldn't. So why dwell on it?

"Don't tell me," Lex went on. "Your boyfriend's car broke down?"

Chloe shook her head. "No boyfriend. Pete Ross was going to partner me, but—"

"I heard what happened. Poor guy," Lex commiserated. "The way Clark tells it, Pete saved Nell Potter's life."

One of Lex's security guards walked past them, doing his best to blend in with the crowd. But his close-cropped hair and the way his chest muscles strained against his tuxedo told everyone in the room who he was.

"I saw the way you were looking at Clark," Lex said suddenly.

Chloe stiffened. "A cat can look at a king," she said tartly. "He's my friend."

"Nothing more?"

Chloe flushed, but held his gaze. "Nothing more." She caught a glimpse of Renata over Lex's shoulder, and decided to turn this around. "Aren't you neglecting your girlfriend? Won't she mind you talking to me?"

"Not at all. I imagine she has plenty to keep her occupied."

He turned to look. Renata was surrounded by at least a

dozen lettermen, who were hanging on her every word. And movement, in that tight silk dress.

Touché. Chloe gave Lex a long, hard look. Since visiting Pete, she'd found it hard not to think about Henry Tait and the mystery beast that killed him. Lex was her host, and she didn't want to insult him, but . . .

Tact's never been my strongest point.

"You know," she started, "this whole wild beast theory is very strange. I've seen bears, and wolves—and they didn't look remotely like the creature that attacked Lana's aunt. The question is—what *kind* of beast are we dealing with here?"

Lex's tone became a lot more formal. "You're referring to the fertilizer plant?"

Chloe was impressed. He was quick on the uptake. "A lot of people are worried that the chemicals you use are dangerous."

"Tell me about it." Lex's formality vanished as suddenly as it had appeared. "The plant's been checked out by every environmental agency on the face of the planet, but folks still blame me for everything, from monster tomatoes to mutant crows."

Despite herself, Chloe laughed. "I'm not accusing you," she told him. "But you have to admit, when it comes to weirdness, Smallville is in a league of its own."

"I admit it. I only wish I could explain it."

"You and me both."

Chloe was thinking about the murderous creature that walked like a man but killed like a beast.

She'd have been surprised to know Lex was thinking about Clark Kent.

CHAPTER 18

Saturday night

"I bought you a gift. From Miss Mayfern's."

Lana pulled a small, tissue-wrapped package from her black beaded purse, and pushed it across the oak table to Clark.

"Great minds think alike," he told her, producing a similar though slightly larger package from his jacket pocket. She took it from his hands with a thrill of pleasure. "It's probably the best week's business Miss Mayfern has had in years."

The band had left the gallery to take a well-earned break. Lex had hired a local DJ for the interval, and now the sound of classic rock ballads filled the hall. Several couples were slow-dancing, including Lex and Renata.

"You first."

"A gentleman would never upstage a lady," Clark said. "You first."

"Together, then."

Like children able to focus only on their own excitement, they tore the soft packaging off their gifts. Clark had his opened first, and he held up the silver star tiepin. Colored strobe lights flickered and reflected from its points.

"It's great," he told Lana, slipping it onto his tie. "Thanks."

"A star for a star," she told him, smiling.

Carefully, she unwrapped her own present. She gasped

with delight when she saw it, a silver brooch set with blood red stones in the shape of a heart.

"Miss Mayfern had it salted away someplace. She seemed to think the stones were rubies," Clark said, "but at the price she charged, they have to be cut glass."

"It's gorgeous," Lana breathed. She undid the clasp, and attached the brooch to the shoulder strap of her dress. She adjusted its position, then looked up, finally satisfied.

"Clark Kent, that is the single nicest thing anyone has ever given me."

She half-stood up in her seat, and reached across the table to drape her hand behind Clark's neck. She pulled his head toward her.

And their lips met in a searing kiss.

It was the kiss that did it for Whitney.

Skulking in the alcove, he'd been watching their every move. Dancing together was bad enough. The exchange of gifts made him angry, not least because he suspected Lana had set out to buy that tiepin for him. The fact that Clark had chosen something so pretty for Lana—something Whitney would never have thought of in a thousand years—enraged him even more.

And when he saw them kiss, his fury got the better of him.

Balling both his fists, he went charging onto the dance floor.

Out of the corner of his eye, Clark saw someone coming fast toward him.

Instinctively, he drew back from Lana and leapt to his feet, turning to face his attacker. But Whitney was on him before he could defend himself, striking Clark hard in the chest with his shoulder.

Clark staggered back, his feet tangling in the chair he'd been sitting in. Both went crashing to the floor.

"Whitney!" Lana screamed. "Stop it!"

Lana tried to grab his arm, but Whitney shrugged her off. Ignoring her protests, he gave Clark no time to recover. Even as Clark struggled to his feet, Whitney dived at him, his right fist swinging. It exploded against Clark's face, and stars flashed before his eyes.

Dimly, he felt another blow glancing off his forehead.

Then a security guard's brawny arms grabbed Whitney from behind, lifting the teenager clear off his feet and whirling him away from Clark.

Lana ran over and knelt by Clark's side, cradling his head in her arm. She took a small white kerchief from her purse, and gently dabbed away the blood from around his mouth.

"I'm fine, I'll be all right," Clark muttered, getting to his feet. He felt dazed, and a pulse was throbbing painfully in his head. He seemed to be making a habit of being hit.

He leaned against Lana, dimly aware that Lex's guard was still holding the struggling Whitney, backing him away toward the exit.

"Rod," he heard Lex say, "I hate to be a party pooper, but you ought to take your friend Whitney outside until he calms down."

Rod Gaynor twisted his mouth. He'd been getting along just swell with that waitress. But he nodded reluctantly. "Sure, Lex. Okay if we come back afterward?"

"Just as long as there's no more trouble from Whitney."

Rod and his two companions hurried away after Whitney and the guard.

"I'm sorry about that, Clark," Lex said sincerely.

"Not your fault, pal." Clark held a hand to his lip. It was already starting to puff up. "It's not the first time he's tried it. I should have been ready."

Clark looked imploringly at Lana. "We won't let this spoil our evening, right?" he asked.

She nodded wordlessly.

"Maybe Lex can show me where I can clean up . . . ?"

"This way." Lex started to walk off, and Clark followed. "Back in five minutes, Lana."

The kitchen door flew open, and one of the waitresses burst in.

"There's a fight in the hall," she exclaimed, clearly excited by the prospect.

Martha looked up from the burgers she was grilling. "How terrible."

The waitress loaded her tray with cups of fruit juice. "It's the Lang girl's boyfriend." She giggled. "Both of them."

"Clark?" Martha gasped.

She whipped off her apron. "Look after the grill," she ordered, pushing past the startled girl and out of the room.

Clark followed Lex up a spiral stairway to a small bathroom on a mezzanine floor. The decor was pristine white marble, with a single antique Persian plaque depicting angels and lions in the center of one wall.

"Shee! What a mess."

Clark stared at his reflection in the mirror on the wall, as Lex started to run the taps. The left side of his mouth was swollen, and his lower lip was puffed and drooping. The collar of his shirt was torn, and there were several buttons missing from its front.

Lex soaked a towel in warm water, wrung it out, and handed it to Clark. "Don't worry. If love really is blind, Lana won't even notice."

Clark winced as he dabbed at his wounds with the damp cloth. "One thing's for sure," he said disappointedly, "she won't be kissing me goodnight!" Lex laughed out loud, and Clark looked askance. "It wasn't that funny."

"No, but you are. Or, rather, *I* am," he quickly corrected

himself. "Ever since you pulled me from that car wreck, I've had my suspicions about you, Clark."

"Suspicions? Like what?" he asked, speaking from the side of his mouth, trying to favor his lip. "You think I'm a serial killer, or something?"

"Far from it, bud. But I did think maybe there was something . . . different about you. I was convinced my car hit you—but you didn't have so much as a scratch. Then the other night, you got to the kitchen before me—in the pitch dark. You fought with that thing. Quite a lot for one normal teenager, don't you agree?"

Clark felt as if the older man's eyes were trying to peer into his very soul. He remembered everything his mother and father had said to him over the past few days. And now here was Lex coming on with the same sort of crazy nonsense.

"And how's that funny, exactly?" he asked coldly.

"Take another peek in the mirror, pal," Lex suggested. "If you look like that after one round with Whitney Ellsworth, there's no way my car could have hit you! You're as normal as the next guy!"

Clark grunted. "I never doubted that for a moment."

Martha hovered on the edge of the dance floor. A U2 classic blared over the PA system, and more than a hundred teenagers were milling around, impatient for the Mushrooms' second set. There was no sign of Lex, or Clark.

She spotted Lana sitting at a table with Chloe, heads close together, deep in conversation. Martha didn't hesitate, but marched over to join them.

"Excuse me, Lana." Both girls looked up. "I heard something about Clark being involved in a fight. Do you know where he is?"

Chloe grimaced, and got up from her seat. "I was just going, Mrs. Kent," she said. "Lana will tell you everything."

Martha sat down in Chloe's place. The waitresses would be running out of food soon, but that was too bad. Her son came first.

She listened as Lana explained about Whitney's assault on Clark, shaking her head and tutting. "Was he hurt?"

"Whitney punched him. His mouth was bleeding."

Wearily, Martha shook her head. Up until a few days ago, Clark wouldn't have been fazed by a punch from the heavyweight champion of the world. What could have changed him so quickly?

She thought back to the only other time she'd ever seen Clark bleed. He'd been exposed to dust from one of the many meteors which still lay buried around the Smallville countryside. Temporarily, he'd lost his incredible abilities. He'd cut himself then, and he was as surprised as she and Jonathan were to see blood on his arm.

Exposure to a meteor might explain his loss of powers, then. But how could he possibly have forgotten that he was ever any other way?

"I feel as if I'm to blame," Lana was saying. "I threw Whitney over for Clark. I guess I should have been more tactful about it. Then maybe Whitney wouldn't have gotten so mad."

"You should never blame yourself for someone else's behavior," Martha said, automatically assuming the role of parent. "We're all responsible people."

Lana smiled. "I see where Clark gets his wisdom from. He once told me that, too."

"Lana—can I ask you a personal question?" A sudden thought had occurred to her, another fragment of the jigsaw that was taking over their lives.

Lana nodded.

"A very personal question?"

Lana's eyes became more guarded, but she nodded again. "I guess."

"Why did you dump Whitney for Clark?" Martha asked. "I mean, you'd been dating Whitney for a year, hadn't you? I always knew that Clark liked you—but from the way he talked, he thought he didn't stand a chance with you."

Lana's cheeks reddened with embarrassment. "I guess it was because—" she began, before her words faltered and faded away. She tried again. "It must have been because—" But again, she couldn't finish the sentence.

She closed her eyes. Her forehead wrinkled, as if she was trying to shut out the music, trying to force herself to remember. Shaking her head, her eyes flicked open again.

"I have to tell you, Mrs. Kent," she said, as evenly as she could, "I don't know why. One day I was happy with Whitney, and the next . . . I don't know, Clark just seemed to become the most important thing in my life."

"Love's like that," Martha admitted. But she would have expected more: for instance, for Lana to say that Clark had a great sense of humor, or that he was reliable, or handsome, or had a sharp, intelligent mind.

Love may be a blind emotion, she thought. *But people almost always try to rationalize it.*

"Did anything happen," Martha went on, "to make you unhappy with Whitney? Did you quarrel? Something your Aunt Nell said, maybe?" She felt like she was clutching at straws, but she knew with fierce certainty there had to be a rational explanation underlying all of this.

"No, Aunt Nell quite likes Whitney." Lana frowned thoughtfully. "And the only other person I spoke to was Miss Mayfern, when I went to her shop. Come to think of," she went on with sudden realization, "I went in to buy a gift for Whitney—and came out with one for Clark." She shrugged. "I guess that was when my feelings must have changed."

Martha felt her pulse quicken. Miss Mayfern! Clark had gone to the old gift shop, too. And it was immediately after that he'd forgotten who he was, and what he could do. But how could a sweet old lady like Violet Mayfern make such a difference to people?

"I haven't seen Violet in years," she went on, trying to keep the conversation alive. "How is she?"

"She seemed quite frail, to look at. But she certainly has her wits about her. We talked for absolutely ages. She's very perceptive, and understanding." Lana smiled, and added as an afterthought: "And she made me the best mint tea I've ever tasted."

Martha's heart almost stopped. She could almost hear the crash as the final piece of the jigsaw fell into place. "*Green* mint tea, by any chance?" she heard herself ask.

"Mm." Lana nodded. "It was the most amazing deep green color. Almost emerald. She grows the herb herself, and uses water from her own well. She should market it— she'd do a lot better than the gift shop does."

Suddenly, Martha Kent *knew*.

CHAPTER 19

Saturday night

The Harley's headlamps blazed into the watery darkness, hurtling through the pelting rain. Ray Dansk could barely make out the road more than twenty yards ahead.

The entrance to the Luthor mansion loomed suddenly out of the night. He braked hard and veered the hog through the open security gates. He gunned the engine and the powerful motorbike careened down the driveway, sending gravel flying.

For the first time in his life, he was playing the part he'd always wanted to play.

The motorcycle outlaw.

The rider on the storm. The ghost rider, who came and went according to his own laws.

The leather-clad loner who struck fear and loathing in the hearts of middle America.

Ray Dansk, Smallville Dragon.

Where the driveway forked, he steered away from the wide terrace with its dozens of parked cars. Instead, he chose the path that led around the back of the castle. He'd noticed something on his last visit that was going to provide him with the perfect entrance.

Every head would turn. Every voice would scream.

"Ray Dansk, Smallville Dragon!"

The turf bank that encircled the castle rose steeply just outside the great hall, inclining in toward the magnificent stained-glass window.

Eyes fixed, teeth bared, water streaming off him, the Smallville Dragon steered the bike toward the incline. He flicked down a gear and opened the throttle as far as it would go.

The bike leaped forward, its front wheel leaving the ground as Dansk pulled back hard on the handlebars. The rear wheel skidded slightly as it hit the grass, and for a moment Dansk thought he was going to crash.

Then the tire recovered its grip, leaving a long, muddy slash in the grass as the bike shot upward into the air.

Ray Dansk screamed in triumph as he arced toward the huge stained-glass window, his voice swallowed up by the clamor of the storm.

The Mushrooms were back on the minstrel's gallery, five heads nodding in unison as they roared through the chorus of their first number.

The dance floor was packed.

One of the running backs had asked Chloe for a dance, and now she regretted having agreed. Her rhythm was completely spoiled as she twisted and swayed to avoid his clumsy feet and swinging arms.

Amazing! This guy can carry a ball fifty yards with the grace of a gazelle. And here he is, making like a windmill.

The strobe lights flashed—red, amber, yellow, white—throwing a never-ending cascade of colors across the dancers. Chloe glanced across at the candlelit tables, where Lana and Mrs. Kent were still talking.

Weird party, she thought. *Typical Smallville!*

There was a sudden bright flash of lightning outside. A roar deeper than thunder cut across the Mushrooms' buzz saw music.

Then the stained-glass window exploded in a million flying shards.

The Harley curved down through the air toward the teenagers below.

Dansk could hear their screams as shattered glass rained down on them. But, blinded by the sudden lights, he lost control of the bike. It skidded as it hit the dance floor, toppling sideways and throwing Dansk off.

He slid, and careened into a terrified teenager, knocking him off his feet. Dansk was sure he heard bone snap.

The bike screeched across the floor on its side, bringing down several dancers too slow to leap aside. Its handlebars buckled, ripping the brakes and mudguard off the front wheel. It ricocheted off a table leg, cracking it in half. Candles and glasses and plates of food went crashing to the floor. The bike skidded on, slamming into a solid stone wall in a bedlam of shrieking metal. Liquid began to spill from the burst fuel tank, and the air filled with the smell of gasoline.

The band had stopped playing, and as their final notes faded away, a momentary silence fell on the hall.

Lightning flashed outside, and a gust of wind sent sheets of rain pouring in through the broken window.

Then a girl screamed, and everyone seemed to be running at once.

If the impact had hurt him, Dansk didn't feel it.

He rolled swiftly to his feet. His plan had never been anything grand, merely to burst in and hurt as many people as possible. Teach Smallville a lesson for what it had done to him. Show the good people of the city what the price was when they tangled with Ray Dansk.

His eyesight was adjusting rapidly, and in the strobe's still-spinning lights, he saw two security guards running at him.

Dansk ducked beneath the first guard's roundhouse punch and brought his hand clawing up to rake across the man's neck and face. Blood spurted, and the guard fell back with a hand to his neck, trying to staunch the flow.

Dansk gave him no time to recover, kicking out at the man's midriff with his heavy motorcycle boots. The guard bent double.

Even as the second guard lunged at him, Dansk leaped forward and used the injured man's shoulders to vault upward. He grabbed on to the ornately carved wooden frieze that ran the entire length of the minstrel's gallery. Hauling himself up, he grabbed the gallery handrail and vaulted over.

As the second guard tried to follow, Dansk leaned down to slash at his head. The man lost his grip and fell back heavily to the dance floor.

The five members of the Mushrooms backed frantically away from their guitars and amplifiers. Dansk snarled as he rushed toward them. Snatching up a chrome-plated microphone stand, he swung it like a battle-ax.

The heavy tripod stand smashed into the lead singer's head. There was a crack as his neck broke. He collapsed onto the drum kit, and the other musicians ran for their lives. Dansk threw the heavy stand at their retreating backs.

He grabbed the largest of the fallen drums and hurled it over the gallery handrail. It crashed to the floor below, narrowly missing a sobbing teenage girl nursing a badly cut leg.

Dansk roared, and began to lob electric guitars and amplifiers over the parapet.

When the window smashed, Martha had been sitting with Lana, tactfully trying to pump her for more information about Violet Mayfern. They were seated a little off to one side, and the fragments of glass that flew through the air didn't reach them.

Then the hall was seething with terrified people, all trying to get out of the way of the crazed beast that had fallen from the motorbike. Martha saw it tussle with the guards, then clamber up onto the gallery.

A drum soared through the air. It arced down to strike a fleeing dancer in the small of the back, sending him sprawling facefirst to the floor.

For the first time, Martha realized that Chloe had been hurt. The girl was sitting in the middle of the dance floor, surrounded by broken equipment, blood streaming from her arm where a shard of glass had slashed her.

Without thinking of her own safety, Martha ran out onto the floor. She dodged aside as a heavy amplifier sailed down toward her, trailing electric cables. It exploded close to her feet, showering her with debris.

She grabbed Chloe from behind, and started to pull her away from the danger area. She could see that the girl was pale and in shock. Blood oozed between her fingers where she clutched her injured arm.

An electric guitar curled through the air, narrowly missing Martha's head before it crunched into the wall, bringing down an oriental tapestry.

The next drum that was thrown fell short, and Martha breathed a sigh of relief as she realized they were out of range.

Dansk lifted the Mushrooms' heavy mixing console, yanking its lead from the socket in a shower of blue sparks. Wavering under its weight, he carried it to the parapet and toppled it over. He was rewarded by a destructive crash as it landed on the remains of the Harley Davidson.

It was then he saw her—the girl sitting petrified against the wall. She'd been at the Potter place the other night. She deserved to suffer for what they'd put him through. He remembered the taste of bleach in his mouth and spit through his teeth.

Growling and snarling, Dansk vaulted onto the gallery

parapet and balanced precariously. He drew back his arms and leaped, curling through the air toward the heavy wrought iron chandelier hanging from the vaulted ceiling.

His momentum caused the chandelier to lurch and move. As it reached the apex of its swing, Dansk jumped.

Lana screamed, and drew back in terror as the monster landed on the oak table in front of her. He teetered for a moment before recovering his balance, then his hand swept down toward her in a savage backhand blow. His fist struck her head, and Lana groaned.

His hand grabbed her hair, and through a red haze she could see his fingers curling like talons on his other hand, as he drew it back for a death blow.

The castle's stone walls—up to ten feet thick in places—effectively muffled all sound.

It wasn't until Clark and Lex reached the foot of the spiral staircase that they realized something was drastically wrong. More than a dozen teenagers were running along the hallway in frenzied panic, desperate to get away.

Lex grabbed a passing teenager by the arm, and yanked him to a halt. "What is it?" he demanded. "What's going on?"

"Somebody's freaked out in the hall," the teenager gasped. "He's hurting people!"

Lex let him go, and broke into a run toward the great hall. "Call the police!" he yelled back over his shoulder, as the young man turned to flee again.

Clark ran after Lex, and they arrived at the hall entrance together. They stopped dead in their tracks, hardly able to believe the sight that greeted them.

The huge window was smashed beyond repair. Piles of

broken glass littered the dance floor. Smashed and broken
musical instruments were scattered everywhere. Yellow
flames were starting to lick from the wrecked motorbike
lying in a tangle against the wall. Renata and a dozen terrified teenagers hugged the walls, too afraid to flee.

Lex hurried to an alcove and grabbed a fire extinguisher
from its cradle. The flames were spreading to a tapestry
hanging on the wall, and if he couldn't douse them, the
whole castle might go up in flames.

"I'll get the others out," Clark shouted, ignoring the pain
in his jaw, as Lex raced toward the fast-growing fire.

It was then that Clark saw Lana. She was slumped
against a wall, trapped on her seat by the refectory table in
front of her. Standing on the table, clawed hand raised to
strike, was the beast he'd faced the other night.

This was the first time he'd seen it properly. As tall as a
man, it looked like a giant, tailless lizard. Its skin was covered in hard, scaly skin that had a greenish tinge to it. Its
eyes glittered fiery red, and saliva dripped from its fangs and
ran down its jaw.

"No!" The word burst from Clark's mouth. He found
himself running without having made any conscious decision to do so. He flung himself full-length in a football
tackle even Whitney would be proud of.

His outstretched arms took the beast around the waist, the
momentum of his dive sending them both hurtling to the
floor. Clark landed on top of his opponent and tried to ce-
ment his advantage by pinioning his arms to the floor.

But the beast was strong. It ripped one arm free, and its
elbow stabbed up to jab Clark in the face. In exactly the
same spot that Whitney had hit. Clark yelped as white-hot
pain seared through him, and the beast easily shrugged him
off.

Scrambling to its feet, the monster kicked out at Clark.

The heavy motorcycle boot took him in the ribs with such force that he was sent sliding across the floor. He felt his jacket shredding as he skidded over broken glass. He heard Renata scream, then his head slammed against a table leg, and he knew no more.

Lex struck the extinguisher's knob hard against the floor, and directed the jet of fast-expanding foam at the flames licking from the wrecked motorbike. A tapestry on the wall above had started to smolder, and now it burst into flame.

Lex drenched the whole area in foam, and the flames flickered and died as their oxygen supply was stifled.

He whirled around as he heard Clark's anguished roar, just in time to see his friend dive at the beast. But the beast knew how to fight, and Clark didn't. Even as it kicked out at Clark, Lex was running across the floor.

"Try this for size," he yelled.

As the monster swung around to face this new attacker, Lex restarted the extinguisher's jet. A flood of foam spurted into the beast's face, forcing its way into its nose and eyes and mouth. It clawed frantically at its face, trying to wipe the suffocating chemicals away.

The jet gave out with a sudden spurt of liquid.

Lex didn't hesitate. He swung the metal extinguisher like a club, and grunted with satisfaction as it thudded into solid flesh.

The beast let out a scream, and Lex swung again.

But this time his foe was ready. It lurched back from the wild blow, and the canister whistled past its chest. Before Lex could regain his balance for another attempt, it kicked upward. Its boot connected with Lex's groin.

The billionaire's son fell forward to the floor, effectively paralyzed by the blow.

"Clark! Clark, you have to wake up!"

Martha knelt by her unconscious son, slapping his face in a desperate attempt to bring him around.

She'd heard his outraged scream cut through the noise and chaos in the hall. Pausing only to be sure Chloe was all right, she'd rushed across the dance floor to her injured son's side. Glancing up, she saw a pitcher full of iced water, miraculously sitting unspilled on an undamaged table. She snatched it up, and dashed the contents into Clark's face.

Clark came to, spluttering and groaning.

"Wh-what happened?" he stammered. He felt strange, confused and bewildered, unable to make sense of anything. His mind raced with thoughts, too many and too fast to pin down.

He tried to get up, but his mother held him fast.

"Listen to me, Clark," she hissed urgently. "You have to remember who you really are! Your friends need you. You must remember. You *must!*"

Clark stared at her, his eyes blinking rapidly as he tried to focus. Strange visions swam before him. A child lifting a heavy sack. A teenager running faster than a speeding car.

"I think you've been *hypnotized,*" Martha was saying. "You've forgotten who you are—and what you can do!"

The visions came faster. A boy staring right through a brick wall. An X-ray flash of a human body. Green stones that stole his energy and left him helpless.

Martha tried one final time. "The mint tea Miss Mayfern gave you—I think it contained something from the meteors. You must remember! That monster's going to kill Lex and Lana!"

Clark felt as if he were flickering between two different realities. His head pounded. He thought he saw a spaceship. He felt cold water on his skin. He was pulling a horse from a swamp. The strobe lights flashed. He was curled up in pain as he touched the beast's body. He was in Lana's arms, locked in a passionate embrace.

Remember! Remember who you really are!

And suddenly, everything came flooding back.

His headache disappeared as he sprang to his feet. His numb and bloated lips started to tingle, and he knew his injuries were healing already.

He flexed his muscles and rejoiced at the incredible strength that flowed through him.

Lex Luthor was motionless on the floor, face down. The beast was standing over him, foot raised in the air, ready to stamp down hard on the unconscious Lex's head.

Clark shot forward so fast, the blur of his movement was lost in the flashing of the strobes.

CHAPTER 20

Saturday night

Clark slammed into the beast with the force of a battering ram.

The impact carried them away from Lex as they skidded across the floor together, and smashed through a doorway.

Clark did his best to hold on to his foe's squirming body, but at such close quarters he was badly affected by the meteorite's dark powers, which were running strong through the monster's blood. Pain seared his hands where he gripped it, traveling in writhing waves up his arms and into his torso. His heartbeat faltered and began to thump irregularly.

A squall of rain blew in through the broken window, drenching them, and for the briefest of moments Clark's agony eased. He renewed his struggle to keep hold of the beast, but it was punching and kicking, determined to force Clark to release his grip. Each time a blow landed, Clark's flesh burned, and every nerve in his body spasmed.

A heavy boot caught him in the ribs, and Clark almost passed out at the explosion of pain.

His fingers loosened their grasp.

Winded, feeling as if he'd broken at least one rib, Ray Dansk seized his chance.

With a final tug, he broke free of the teenager's hands. He whirled on one foot, his other powering in to deliver another kick to the midriff.

He recognized this creep, too—another of those who'd tried to stop him when he went after the Potter woman. Another fool marked for death.

"Clark—no!" a woman screamed, and began to run toward him. Shrugging off the pain in his chest, Dansk stooped to grab up a guitar lying on the floor, one he'd previously hurled down from the gallery. Holding it by the neck, brandishing it like an ax, he hurled it at his new assailant.

As it cleaved through the air toward her, Martha Kent's foot slipped in the wrecked components of an amplifier. She fell heavily to the floor, and the guitar passed harmlessly over her head.

The teenage girl Dansk had targeted was slumped in her chair. He moved closer to her—only to be sent flying sideways as a figure lunged at him. They fell to the floor, locked together.

Another teenager wanting to be a hero. Wanting to die.

Fighting back his growing weakness and howling with rage, Dansk fought his way free. He lurched to his feet and grabbed his attacker by an arm and a leg. Exerting all his strength, he lifted the teenager bodily off the floor and sent him hurtling through the air to smash against a wall.

Whitney Fordman collapsed in a heap.

Scrambling over the table, Dansk loomed over Lana. The flashing strobe lights gave the scene a surreal feel, his body seeming to move in jerks. Turning his head away from the lights, he snatched the girl up roughly and slung her over one shoulder like a sack of corn.

He turned to the window, using his free hand to knock away the jagged pieces of glass still protruding from the broken frame. Then he summoned up all of his energy, and leaped.

His jump carried him onto the broad window ledge. Without pausing, he leaped again, out through the window.

He almost fell as he landed on the grassy bank outside.

But he recovered his balance, and with the girl still slumped over his shoulder, he staggered away into the driving rain.

Lightning flashed.

Through the remains of the medieval window, a scene of carnage was illumined. At least half a dozen teenagers lay injured on the glass-strewn floor. The two security guards were still and unmoving.

Lex Luthor groaned softly as he struggled to sit up on the floor.

A peal of thunder echoed.

Whitney Fordman had propped himself against a wall. His eyes were wide with pain and shock. Blood trickled from his nose, and his scalp hurt where the beast had torn out a handful of his hair.

Another bolt of lightning filled the room with ethereal light.

Chloe sat on the floor with her head between her knees. The makeshift tourniquet Martha had applied had stanched the flow of blood, but she felt weak, and dizzy, and exhausted. As if she'd just run ten miles against the clock.

Renata Meissen crouched next to her. Her white silk dress was smeared with blood.

Thunder rolled.

Martha Kent was pulling herself to her feet, wincing at the pain in her ankle. It had twisted as she fell, and it felt like it might give at any moment as she hobbled over to where Clark lay in a scattering of colored glass.

Now that the source of her son's vulnerability had been removed, he recovered rapidly from the meteor's debilitating effects.

"Thank the Lord you're all right." She wrapped her arms around Clark, and hugged him tight. If she'd lost him—

She didn't allow herself to finish the thought.

Lightning flashed.

"Where's Lana?" Clark wanted to know.

Martha's voice was low and afraid. "That beast took her."

Face set grimly, Clark began to stride away. Martha gripped his arm.

"Clark, you can't go after it," she said urgently. "You know what contact with it did to you. Next time, you could die!"

"But I can't just leave her!"

To Martha, the thunder that reverberated through the hall sounded like a death knell.

Clark's mind raced as he ran through the possibilities. They all ended the same way—with him helpless, at the mercy of the monster.

Out of the corner of his eye, he saw Whitney walk shakily toward him. Whitney held one hand to the back of his head, and his eyes were screwed half-shut with pain.

"Lana . . . ?" he asked.

Clark shook his head. "That . . . thing ran away with her."

Whitney groaned. "I know this isn't the time or the place, Kent," he muttered, "but I want to tell you I'm sorry. I behaved like a jerk. I saw you trying to save Lex." Clark saw shame on his face. "I misjudged you."

"Let's worry about that later. The important thing right now is Lana . . ."

He broke off in sudden realization. Lead was the only substance that seemed to protect him from the meteors' emanations.

And there was a four-foot lead cross hanging on a wall not far away.

Lex had come over to join them, and Martha quickly told him what had happened to Lana.

"The police should be on their way," he said, "but we can't afford to wait for them. We can use the cars to search."

"I'm for that," Whitney agreed quickly. "Kent?"

"I'll join you. There's something I have to do first."

"Stay here," Clark told his mother, as Lex and Whitney and the other lettermen hurried away. "Look after Chloe, and anyone else who's hurt."

"What are you going to do?"

"Don't worry. I have an idea."

"Please, be careful," Martha begged, as he strode out into the hallway.

When he was sure there was nobody else around, Clark accelerated to superspeed. He raced through the halls, a human blur, and a second later halted beneath the ancient Byzantine cross.

Quickly, he pulled it off its mountings. Glancing around to make sure he was still alone, he grasped the arms of the crucifix and squeezed. The pressure produced by his strength buckled the lead. It crumpled, and he rolled it into a large, irregular ball.

Fleetingly, it crossed his mind that he was destroying a priceless, and probably irreplaceable, artifact. But human life was worth more than anything, no matter how valuable.

Placing the rough lead ball on the floor, he began to pound it at superspeed. Dozens of blows per second rapidly flattened the pliable metal against the flagstoned floor.

The lead spread out in an ever-growing sheet, thinning as it widened.

Satisfied with his handiwork, Clark rolled the quarter-inch-thick lead sheet into a cylinder.

He could guess where the beast had gone. According to a police statement on the radio, Ray Dansk had been hiding out in the caves beneath the Durban Street bluff.

If his mother's theory was right, Miss Mayfern had given Clark mint tea with traces of meteorite in it. The old lady had been proud of having her own well. If her contaminated water had percolated down through the rock to the caverns below, that would explain what had happened.

There was no beast. Only Ray Dansk, his mind and body warped by contact with the meteorites.

The caves were the most likely source of his weird power.

That's where he'd be heading.

Clark gathered up the lead bundle under one arm and began to run.

He passed a bicycle leaning against a wall and was a rain-soaked blur as he streaked past the throng of wet people milling around in the parking area of the castle. They seemed to have slowed down to a fraction of their normal speed, and Clark heard Whitney say:

"My truck, man! The creep's stolen my truck!"

Other vehicles were starting up, their lights flaring into life, piercing the lashing rain.

Clark ran on.

In the distance, he could hear police cars and ambulances, their sirens wailing above the crash of the tempest.

Then he was speeding past the approaching emergency vehicles, out of the driveway and onto the road, racing through the rain toward the watery lights of Smallville.

"May the good Lord preserve us!"

Sheriff Bryan Shugrue stood in the castle's great hall, outraged by the scale of the destruction. Paramedics were carrying out the injured on stretchers or helping support those who could still walk.

He recognized one of the girls—she'd been at Nell Potter's the other night. What was her name again? Sullivan.

Her arm was heavily bandaged, and she looked paler than a ghost.

Martha Kent was sitting with her ankle resting on a bench, holding an ice pack to it.

A wrecked motorcycle lay against a fire-scarred wall, smothered in foam. Tables and chairs lay upended everywhere, and the floor was a sea of broken glass.

And the man responsible for the chaos and destruction was getting away.

Shugrue roared to his deputies, and they all hurried back out into the storm.

I was right! They're here!

Clark slowed to a halt halfway down a path in Riverside Park. Whitney's pickup truck lay a hundred yards away, buried up to the axle in churned mud and grass. It had been abandoned, with the engine running and its lights still burning.

Clark shot down to the riverbank and stealthily approached the entrance to the caves. He stooped under the barrier that said POLICE LINE—DO NOT CROSS, and contemplated the cave entrance.

The boards had been ripped away in places, where the police had broken through. He defocused his eyes, bringing his X-ray vision into play. He ought to be able to see right through the cliff wall, into the cave.

But the stone was thick, and contaminated by long exposure to meteor-infected water.

He could see nothing except darkness and twinkling points of green light.

Sighing, Clark began to unroll the sheet of lead.

He just hoped this was going to work . . . !

Dansk lay flat on the cave floor, his breathing fast and ragged. It had taken every last ounce of his strength to drag the girl into the caves. She was still unconscious, lying in the damp moss just inside the entrance.

He was exhausted. He needed nourishment, and he needed it fast.

Forcing himself to move, he crawled toward the wall containing the entrance to the upper chamber. Every fiber of his body ached and screamed its dissent. Twice, his foot slipped on the rock as he tried to pull himself up. He was on the point of admitting defeat and falling to the floor, when his hand caught the sill.

With renewed vigor, painfully he hauled himself up.

He threw himself down in the pool of water on the chamber floor, sucking it greedily into his mouth. He lay down in it and rolled over, his hands splashing it all over his body.

And he felt life flood back into him. Energy ripped through him, surging in his veins like electricity.

The dragon tattoo undulated across his chest. He could feel its fiery eyes blazing out from his flesh.

The snarl was back on his mouth as he slithered toward the exit.

There was a girl who had to suffer. . . .

Clark felt like one of the medieval knights whose suits of armor were displayed inside Lex's gatehouse.

The sheets of lead were wrapped around his torso, fused together by his strength. His chest and back were completely covered, but he'd left his elbows, knees, and neck free so he could move comfortably.

He tried to mold a sheet as a mask, around his face, but it hampered him too much. And besides, in the same way that it blocked the meteors' radiation, lead also blocked his X-ray vision.

He kept the two smallest sheets for last, wrapping them around his hands like boxing gloves.

Gritting his teeth, Clark charged through what was left of the barrier boards.

The cave's meteor-tinged darkness was still impervious to his vision.

But a bolt of lightning split the sky, and Clark saw Lana in its flickering light. She lay in a crumpled heap on a patch of moss, looking young and pathetic and totally helpless. Clark felt a lump rise in his throat.

Thunder began to roll as the lightning faded. Clark caught a glimpse of the beast, dropping down from a gap higher up the wall, growling and snarling. It looked more dangerous than ever.

Then the light was gone.

"Give yourself up," Clark said threateningly into the darkness. "Don't force me to hurt you."

He heard a series of guttural grunts, as if the monster was trying to speak, but failing.

Then it leaped through the air at him in a frenzy of slashing claws.

Protected by his lead armor, the effects of his enemy's proximity to Clark were minimal. He felt faintly nauseous, but his strength wasn't fading as it normally would. Clark punched out with one lead-lined fist and felt it connect with flesh. The beast shot back against the cave wall.

Before Clark could reorient himself, it lowered its head and charged. The top of its head caught Clark in his unprotected face. His nerves jangled painfully. It was a hundred times worse than being struck by Whitney.

Then claws ripped out at his chest, gouging right through the lead sheeting. Where the claws touched Clark's flesh, agony flared.

He fell back, away from the source of his pain. But the cavern seemed to be redolent with the uncanny meteor, as if tiny grains of it floated in the dampness in the air. He was finding it increasingly hard to breathe, and his eyes were starting to burn.

He had to get this over with, fast.

Yet how could he, when he couldn't see his opponent?

Clark flailed blindly around him, lead-sheathed fists striking only air. Obviously, the beast could see in the dark, because none of the wild blows even touched it.

Clark stopped swinging. Standing perfectly still, he tuned in his acute hearing. Affected by the meteorite dust in the cave, he could hear popping and fizzing coming from nowhere.

But he also heard quiet breathing, moving around him a couple of yards away. The cavern was large enough for the beast to hug the wall and get behind Clark. That was obviously what it was trying to do.

Instinctively, Clark spun through 180 degrees, and shot out his fist in a textbook straight right.

Lightning rent the air. In a series of flicker-fast images, he saw his fist explode into a hideous, snarling face. The sheer force of the blow lifted the beast clear off its feet.

As the light from outside started to die away, Clark hit out with a left hook that crashed into his enemy's jaw.

The monster fell to the slimy floor and lay there twitching and gasping.

But Clark's triumph was short-lived.

A green, twinkling mist seemed to be forming around him, sapping his strength, fragmenting his thoughts. His whole body was suffering low-level pain, with hotspots around his chest and the joints he hadn't covered in lead. It was getting harder to move. Harder to think.

He fell to his knees and quickly ripped the lead shielding off one hand. It immediately started to throb. Biting back the pain, Clark grabbed Lana's arm. He jerked into a half-upright position and struggled valiantly to lift her.

His muscles were starting to seize up, and his eyes could see nothing except pinpricks of flashing green light.

With one final effort, he hoisted Lana's sagging body in his arms. He stumbled forward, one pace, two . . . then his foot skidded on the slippery moss. He fell forward against the cave wall and felt the lead sheet ripping from his arm.

Then he was outside, and toppling, still trying to hold on to Lana.

They landed on wet grass and rolled, coming to a halt on the lip of the riverbank.

CHAPTER 21

Saturday night

"That's Whitney Fordman's truck!"

Deputy Morrison sent the patrol car tooling down the park path. It was barely wide enough to take the vehicle, and he veered around corners, leaving deep skid marks in the grass.

"Looks like it's stuck in mud," Sheriff Shugrue noted from the passenger seat, peering out his window through the heavy rain that still beat down. "Park right here."

They got out of the car and slipped their pistols from their holsters. It was hard to see, the rain was so heavy, driven by the gusting wind.

A blaze of headlamps heralded the arrival of a half-dozen other vehicles, including Lex and Whitney in the Porsche. They'd covered miles of the back roads, seeing no sign of the beast or his victim. When they saw the sheriff's car heading for town, its siren whooping, they decided to follow.

As teenagers started to pile out of the cars, Shugrue held up a hand. "Stay back," he warned. "I don't want any of you getting hurt!"

He gestured to Morrison and set out across the sodden turf, his boots sinking up to the ankles. Gun held ready, Morrison followed him through the deluge.

Clark had crossed the river and propped Lana against the trunk of a willow tree that jutted from the bank on the far side. Her flimsy dress was soaked through, and there were patches of mud on her arms and legs. But as far as he could tell, her pulse and breathing seemed fine. At least the tree's branches would provide a little shelter from the downpour.

His lead armor was ripped and shredded, parts of it torn away completely. Clark glanced toward the cave and set his jaw determinedly. He was going to have to go back in, and—somehow—bring the monster out.

He smoothed out his lead wrappings as best he could. He wasn't looking forward to what he had to do. He took one step toward the entrance—

And stopped abruptly.

A massive streak of lightning lit up the whole sky, seeming to come from directly above. It zigzagged through the air and struck the base of the old chestnut tree on top of the bluff.

There was a sharp crack, almost lost in the howling wind. Then slowly, almost reluctantly, the huge tree started to topple. It fell forward with a crash.

Roots that had held the tree for more than a century ripped from the ground. The sodden soil offered little resistance, and the roots tore out boulders and huge lumps of earth. They went cascading down the cliff face, with the mighty tree trunk rolling behind them.

Suddenly, half the bluff was moving. Loosened by the torrential rain, it slipped away from Durban Street, thousands of tons of earth and stone plunging in an unstoppable avalanche.

Through the rain, Clark could make out the beast staggering from the cave. It looked up, and even from this distance Clark could see the look of horror on its face as it realized the whole cliff was coming down on it.

Clark accelerated instantly to superspeed.

Rocks and boulders ricocheted off his body as he reached the cave. He'd grown used to never hurting himself, but he'd never tested his power to see just how invulnerable he might be.

He found out now, as huge rocks smashed against him, sending him spinning away. He swung one arm, ripping it free of its armor, and sent a car-sized boulder exploding away from him.

Then he had the beast in his arms. His body flooded with pain, and the rain of rocks and earth and branches around him had become a torrent trying to beat him to the ground. He couldn't allow that to happen. If he fell now, he might never get up again.

He held it to him, as tightly as he dared. Pain haunted every movement. Flexing his legs, he propelled himself up and away with all the strength that he had.

A plunging boulder shattered as it plummeted into his back. Then he was soaring through the rocky downpour, and into clear air.

More by luck than design, they splashed down in the river.

The landslide continued, pouring over the cave mouth, sweeping away the barriers. Rocks bounced and careered across the grass into the water. The huge chestnut tree had been reduced to matchwood.

Then everything was still. The storm was moving away.

Clark hauled himself onto the riverbank, dragging his captive behind him. Even as he gazed down at the unconscious form, it began to change.

The sharp fangs drew back into its gums, and its claws retracted into its fingertips. Its scaly hide seemed to shimmer, and the lizardlike scales changed back into human skin.

As the fiery red glow died from its eyes, Clark found himself staring down at a man.

By the time Sheriff Shugrue reached the riverbank, the rain had almost stopped.

Ray Dansk lay sprawled unconscious on the riverbank.

And thirty yards away, Clark Kent knelt by the body of Lana Lang.

"Lana. Lana, speak to me."

He cradled her head in his arms, stroking her face gently, wiping away the drips that fell from the leaves above. She looked so defenseless, he wanted to spend the rest of life protecting her.

Clark had stripped off what remained of his lead armor as he hurried back to Lana's side, tossing it into the river as he ran. The less evidence he left of his actions tonight, the better for all concerned.

He was aware of people coming toward him—Lex, and Whitney, and a gang of other kids. There were no lights in this part of the park, he reassured himself. The rain had been almost impenetrable. Nobody could possibly have seen what he'd done.

"Uuuh." Lana stirred. Her eyelids fluttered open. She tried to sit up, but the effort was too much, and she sank back against his arms.

"I . . . I feel like I've been dreaming," she murmured, her eyes blinking and unfocused. "I can't tell what's real, and what isn't. . . ."

"It was a nightmare," Clark said gently. "And we were all in it."

She stared up at his face, as if seeing him for the first time. Clark frowned as she gave a visible start.

"Oh no!" she exclaimed. And then: "Where's Whitney?"

Clark's heart sank like a lead balloon.

Numbly, he straightened up. Whitney walked past him, looking away, not meeting his eyes.

Clark glanced back to see Whitney had taken his place by Lana's side. She gazed deeply into his eyes and held his hand as if she never wanted to let it go.

Ironic, Clark thought. *Here's me figuring I was her knight in shining armor. But I guess I was just a klutz wrapped in sheets of lead.*

His jacket and shirt hung in tatters, and somewhere along the line he'd lost a shoe.

Hunching his shoulders, he limped away.

"Don't be leaving the country, Kent," the sheriff called as Clark walked past him. "I'll be needing a witness statement from you."

"Tomorrow okay?"

"Sure." The sheriff's voice softened. "You go home and get some rest. You look like you could use it."

Bryan Shugrue finished cuffing Dansk's hands behind his back. The man was still unconscious, looking pale and shriveled and bedraggled, more like a rat than a human being. None of his bones seemed to be broken, but he was definitely in a bad way.

Shugrue wasn't taking any chances. He cuffed Dansk's ankles, too.

"Call an ambulance," he ordered Morrison. "Lord knows, he doesn't deserve it, after everything he's done. But a man's innocent until he's proven guilty ... even this psycho."

He looked across the river, at what was left of the Durban Street bluff.

"Get Martin or somebody to go up there and check out Miss Mayfern," he added. "Looks like half her backyard took the plunge. She's lucky the house is still there."

The bluff was unrecognizable now, the hoary old chestnut gone, a town landmark that would never be seen again. Half the bluff itself had caved in, completely burying the cavern and partly blocking the river. Perched on top, like something Alfred Hitchcock might have staged, was Miss Mayfern's Gothic house.

"I hope you're happy, big shot," Shugrue snarled with contempt at the unhearing Dansk. "Last of the Smallville Dragons."

"Taxi, sir?"

Lex appeared at Clark's side, gesturing toward the silver Porsche waiting at the park entrance. "I'll take you home."

"No." Clark shook his head. "Your place. Mom's still there."

Lex led the way toward his car.

Incredible, Clark thought incongruously. *After all this— even in the rain—he looks impeccable. His clothes are ripped, and he's still the best-dressed guy in town!*

They got into the car, and Lex started the engine. If he was suffering from his injuries, he didn't mention it.

Clark's thoughts returned to Lana.

Maybe it's a fair trade. I save your life, you break my heart. He tried to rationalize his feelings. *If Mom's right, and Miss Mayfern hypnotized Lana, then she never really loved me anyway. It was just a sham—like me believing I'd lost my powers.*

And both of us were taken in. We were both living a lie.

The thought didn't cheer him one little bit.

Still shaken by the night's events, Lex drove much more sedately than he was used to. The villain had been caught. The urgency was gone. No need to hurry.

"How are you feeling?" He glanced sideways at his passenger.

"Gloomy. Miserable. Despairing. Mix 'n' match." Clark didn't look round, staring vacantly out through the windshield. The rain had stopped completely, leaving large puddles at the sides of the road.

"You have to learn to control those emotions, pal. If Lana is the girl for you, you'll come together one day. No matter what obstacles stand in your way."

"Yeah," Clark said flatly, "and Santa Claus lives on the Moon."

"Hey, everybody knows it's the Arctic Circle!"

Lex sneaked another glance and saw that Clark managed a weak smile. He turned the car off the road, into the castle driveway.

"Two questions for you, tiger," he said as he brought the car smoothly to a halt. "What happened to the split lip?"

Clark put a hand to his mouth. "I don't know." He shrugged. "Maybe contact with cold water eased the swelling."

"Maybe." Lex looked askance, but might have been prepared to let it pass. If it hadn't been for his second question. "How did you get to the park so quickly? I mean, we left you with your mother in the castle. I admit, we didn't drive straight there—but you didn't even have a car."

Clark shrugged again, his face expressionless. "There was a bike parked round back," he said truthfully. "And I know a shortcut." He didn't give Lex time to think of anything else to ask. "Come on. I want to make sure my mom and Chloe are okay."

"Amen to that, pal."

But as he ushered Clark before him to the gatehouse, his eyes narrowed. Maybe Clark was just teasing him. Or maybe he did have a perfectly rational explanation. Or maybe Lex was right to have his suspicions, after all.

It was a mystery.

And sooner or later, Lex would solve it.

"Darling, you were so brave!"

Renata ran to Lex's side. He held her at arm's length, looking her up and down. The front and side of her white dress were streaked with blood, and her eyes were red from crying.

"Are you hurt?"

Renata shook her head. "I was trying to help one of the boys who was talking to me," she said. "His leg was badly gashed by flying glass."

"Is he—?"

"They took him away in an ambulance. They said he'd be all right."

She threw herself suddenly into his arms, hugging him tight. "I thought—I thought you were going to die," she said, fighting back her sobs. "I thought we all were."

"There," Lex hushed her, stroking her long blond hair. "Take it easy. Everything's going to be all right."

The Mushrooms' lead singer, and one security guard had died. The other guard was hospitalized with facial injuries.

Fourteen teenagers in all were taken to hospital, including Chloe, the majority of them cut by flying glass. One had a broken leg. Two of them were on the critical list.

Lex gazed around the great hall, taking in the damage and destruction.

But that didn't matter.

Only people mattered.

Jonathan was waiting anxiously at the door when Martha's car finally pulled up, and she and Clark spilled out.

"Holy Moses," he spluttered, seeing the state Clark was in.

And then he noticed that Martha was limping.

"Are you two all right?"

"We got off lightly compared with some," Martha said somberly. "Two people were killed. And Chloe's being kept in the hospital overnight, for observation."

Martha had called him from the castle to let him know what was going on. He'd wanted to go over there right away, but she'd dissuaded him. So he'd spent the worst two hours of his life pacing the floor waiting for them to get back.

Clark told them both what had happened at the caves. How he'd rescued Lana, only for her to snap back to the way she'd been previously. In love with Whitney.

"I'd better visit Miss Mayfern in the morning," Clark said. "She needs to realize that what she's doing can be dangerous."

"In more ways than one," Martha added ruefully.

"You know, when I think back," Clark went on, "it wasn't as if she deliberately hypnotized me. It was more . . . well, she brought out my deepest feelings. I wanted to be normal, and with the help of her mint tea, she made me normal. But I don't think she knew she was doing it."

"If it is her tea that's contaminated," Jonathan suggested, "she's probably been drinking it herself for years. Maybe it brought out her deepest feelings, too."

"Whatever that was," Martha commented.

"To make people happy." Clark sighed. "She only wanted to make people happy."

CHAPTER 22

Sunday

When Clark turned up at noon, Miss Mayfern wasn't home.

He hardly recognized Durban Street, with the big tree and a whole row of back gardens missing. There was a massive, jagged rent where the bluff had split.

A sheriff's patrol car blocked the road, and engineers in hardhats were swarming over the site.

"The residents have been evacuated until we can declare the area safe," a deputy told him. "All except the old lady." He jerked a thumb toward the Gothic house.

"Why?"

"Sheriff sent us up to check her out last night. We found her collapsed. Seems it was the shock of the lightning strike."

"Is she all right?"

"I haven't heard." He turned away. "She's at the medical center."

Lex and Renata stood outside the gatehouse, saying their farewells.

"Are you sure you don't want me to stay?" she whispered.

Lex shook his head. "It wouldn't be a good idea, Renata. Things were great when they were great. Let's just leave it at that."

They watched as Louis Verne drove Lex's limousine

round from the rear of the castle. He got out, opened the rear door, and began to stack Renata's luggage in the trunk.

"Where will you go?" Lex asked her. "Back to Metropolis? The money Dad paid you must be burning a hole in your purse."

Renata looked wistfully at him. "No, not Metropolis. Somehow, it seems to have lost its attractions." She gazed up into his eyes. "You might not believe this, Lex, but I've enjoyed being here. Smallville's not that bad a place."

"Hey, I'm already converted."

"I think I'll head out to the coast." She smiled suddenly. "Remember what we used to do? Hit the airport, and take the first flight with seats—wherever it was going?" He nodded, and she finished: "I think that's exactly what I'll do."

She reached up and kissed him on the cheek. "Thanks for everything, darling."

He kissed her back. "And my thanks to you. You've taught me a valuable lesson about my father . . . even if I'm not sure what it is yet."

Laughing, she got into the rear of the limo. Lex closed the door behind her.

"Keep in touch," she called through the open window, as the car drove off.

Lex stood watching until it was out of sight.

"Well? Am I well?" Miss Mayfern glared at Clark from her hospital bed. "My mind's sharper than yours, boy!"

He'd expected to find her frail and helpless, hooked up to life support. Instead, she was propped up against her pillows, the gleam in her eye as feisty as ever.

"What do you want, anyway? I told you when you bought the brooch—no returns."

"That's not why I'm here, Miss Mayfern."

Clark sat down on the bedside chair, trying to collect his thoughts. He found it difficult to know where to start. How do you tell an old lady that her well is contaminated with something from outer space? Something that can . . . change people. How do you convince her she's been hypnotizing people into doing things they wouldn't normally do?

Miss Mayfern forestalled him. "My garden's gone," she said abruptly. "And my well." A fleeting sadness crossed her face. "I'm going to miss my well. Such lovely, pure water. It made exquisite mint tea."

Clark gave an audible sigh of relief. Whether or not she'd known what she was doing, if the well was gone there would be no more of her special tea.

"They say my house is unstable. I can't go back."

"I'm sorry to hear that," Clark told her. Though he wasn't. "Will you go into the nursing home?"

"Do you think I'm an invalid?" The fire was back in her eyes, and she gave a mischievous grin. "I'm insured. I'm going to buy an apartment at that new seniors' development in the city. I like people. I'll be happy there."

"I'm glad." Clark rose to his feet. "I have to go now. If you let me know your new address, I'll stop by and visit."

"That would be nice."

Clark's hand was on the doorknob when she spoke again.

"You know," she said quietly, "life is full of pain and misery. All I ever wanted was to be happy. But it was denied me. After Alick died, I lost myself in other people. I wanted them to be happy with their lives, in a way that I never was."

He turned and smiled at her. "I understand, Miss Mayfern. And believe me, I know at least one person you made very, very happy."

He left the room, thinking: *Even if it was only for a few short days.*

CHAPTER 23

One week later

It was Saturday afternoon, and the bleachers at Smallville High football field were packed to capacity.

It wasn't a big game—they were just playing the Otsville Lions—but a significant proportion of the town had turned out for it, partly because Principal Kwan had declared the game to be a memorial for Henry Tait. And partly because it was Smallville's first opportunity to appear in public since the capture of Ray Dansk.

In a way, it was a celebration.

Clark sat with his parents and Chloe, with Lex a few rows behind them. Pete Ross had wanted to sit with them, but his parents insisted he stay with his family. He'd been discharged from the hospital only the day before, with strict instructions to rest and not exert himself. The family occupied nearly a whole row on their own.

Chloe's arm had healed well, and the doctors assured her that, given time, the scar would fade. Meanwhile, she was busy writing the story of Lex's party for the *Torch*. The local papers couldn't compete with her on this one. She'd been an eyewitness.

Principal Kwan had announced his intention to make a speech before the game began, and Clark could see him up on the podium, flanked by Sheriff Shugrue.

"The tragic events of the past few weeks are over," the principal's voice boomed through the PA system. "We must grieve for our losses and proceed with our lives. And what better way of starting than by honoring one of the bravest students this school has ever produced?"

The principal raised a hand to his eyes, shielding them from the afternoon sun, and looked searchingly out into the bleachers.

"Peter Ross, please come to the podium."

For a moment, Pete Ross wondered what he'd done wrong.

He looked furtively round him for an escape route, before he realized the principal had used the word "honor."

His parents beamed with pride as he got to his feet and pushed along to the end of the row. His brothers and sisters made enthusiastic comments as he squeezed past them.

"Yowsah! Go the hero!"

"Proud of you, bro'!"

He walked out onto the playing field toward the podium, and spontaneous applause broke out in the stands. He could see Clark and Chloe and Lex, all on their feet, all clapping.

For him.

Sheriff Shugrue took his arm and guided him up the podium steps, then reached to take the microphone from the principal.

"Peter Ross saved a woman—a respected resident of our town—from almost certain death. With no thought for his own safety, he took his life in his hands in order to rescue somebody else. Such courage should not pass unnoticed. And so, on behalf of the Lowell County Sheriff's Office, I would like to present Peter with this citation for bravery above and beyond that expected of him."

He handed Pete a certificate tied with ribbon, and the audience erupted with cheers.

"Speech, speech," he heard voices call.

Bryan Shugrue thrust the microphone at him. Pete took it,

wondering what he was going to say. And then it came to him.

"I'd like to thank my mom and dad, for making me what I am today." He couldn't keep the grin off his face as he added: "And to my brothers and sisters, I'd just like to say—watch your backs, I'm coming through!"

The school band struck up as Pete began the walk back to his seat.

Clark was still on his feet when the cheerleaders began their prematch warmup. Lana looked so cute in her short skirt and Lurex top, leading the girls in their famous Pom-Pom Dance. He stared at her, unable to tear his eyes away, remembering the time they'd spent together.

It was only a week ago, and yet already it seemed like years had passed.

Lana turned suddenly and caught him staring. She smiled warmly.

Then the teams ran out on the field, and the cheerleaders started their chant. "GO, CROWS, GO!"

Lana gave him a broad wink, then turned back to her squad. "GO, CROWS!"

Leading the Smallville team onto the field, Whitney raised one fist in the air, anticipating victory. Clark heaved a sigh and settled back into his seat.

It was going to be a long afternoon.

EPILOGUE

One month later

Clark stood in the second-floor hallway of a new low-rise apartment block and rang the doorbell of number 23.

"Clark Kent, Miss Mayfern," he declared into the security phone.

The door buzzed open, and he entered.

The apartment was brand new, but the furniture and ornaments were antiques from the old house on Durban Street.

The old lady greeted him in the hallway, her face creasing into a smile when she saw the huge bunch of flowers he held out to her.

"To celebrate your new home," he told her.

"Roses and lilies. My favorites." She took the flowers in her hands and smelled them appreciatively. "I'll just go to the kitchen and put them in a vase. Would you like me to make you a mint tea while I'm there?"

A look of horror crossed Clark's face.

"Store-bought, I'm afraid," the old lady went on. "No garden here, you see."

"I'd love a cup," he told her.

She gestured to another door. "Go on through to the sitting room. I'll join you shortly."

Clark pushed the door open—and stared in astonishment.

Lana Lang was sitting on the sofa.

"Clark. I didn't expect to see you here."

He sat down beside her, careful to keep space between them. "Ditto, Lana."

"I thought Miss Mayfern might appreciate a visit."

"Yes. Me too."

He felt awkward and uncomfortable. He'd seen Lana at school every day for the past month, but never alone. Chloe or Pete or Whitney always seemed to be around. His friends had quizzed him mercilessly about the breakup, and the school gossip machine moved into overdrive now that Whitney and Lana were an item again.

But Clark and Lana never had a chance to talk about what happened between them—and he felt too embarrassed to start discussing it now.

He guessed that, like him, Lana remembered everything about their week together. But for her, it must be a complete mystery as to why she had dumped Whitney and fallen so hard for Clark. She knew nothing of the strange powers possessed by the meteor fragments, or how they allowed Miss Mayfern unknowingly to manipulate their emotions.

To his surprise, Lana was looking almost tenderly at him.

"I wish things hadn't happened the way they did, Clark," she said softly. "But I want you to know—I loved every minute I spent with you. You're a really nice guy."

"It was great being with you, too, Lana." He tried to keep his tone even, to hide the raw emotion he was afraid would break through to the surface. "But in the end"—he shrugged nonchalantly, as if to say none of it really mattered—"I guess we can't escape the reality of our lives. We just have to deal with things as best we can."

Lana leaned over and patted the back of his hand. He felt like he'd received an electric shock.

"That's what makes us human, Clark," she said softly.

Human? Clark thought later, on the long walk home from town. *I'm the guy from Planet X.* He smiled to himself. *Still, if Lana thinks I'm human, I must be doing something right.*

It was getting dark, and the first stars started to twinkle, heralds of the endless cosmos that would soon fill the sky from horizon to horizon. No, he wasn't human. He was from out there someplace.

But maybe—just maybe—love is universal.

For a brief moment in time, Lana had been his. Nobody—not even Lana herself—could ever take that away from him.

If Miss Mayfern brought out my deepest feelings, he thought, *then that's what she must have done with Lana, too.*

Which would mean that Lana's deepest passion wasn't for Whitney at all . . . but for Clark.

Which meant that he still stood a chance with her. Someday. Somehow.

It might not be much, in the scheme of things. But Clark knew that it was enough.

There was nobody in sight. He sidestepped off the road, and into the rows of corn.

And he started to run.

ALAN GRANT was born in Bristol, England in 1949. After finishing school, he edited wildlife, romance, and fashion magazines before becoming a freelance writer. With long-time writing partner John Wagner, he scripted Judge Dredd and a dozen other science fiction series for the British comic book publisher 2000 AD. Since 1987 he has written over 200 Batman stories for DC Comics. He is the author of *The Stone King*, a Justice League novel published by Pocket Books. Alan works in a Gothic mansion in the Scottish border country with his wife and guardian angel, Sue.

VISIT WARNER ASPECT
ONLINE!

THE WARNER ASPECT HOMEPAGE
You'll find us at: www.twbookmark.com then by clicking on Science Fiction and Fantasy.

NEW AND UPCOMING TITLES
Each month we feature our new titles and reader favorites.

AUTHOR INFO
Author bios, bibliographies and links to personal websites.

CONTESTS AND OTHER FUN STUFF
Advance galley giveaways, autographed copies, and more.

THE ASPECT BUZZ
What's new, hot and upcoming from Warner Aspect: awards news, bestsellers, movie tie-in information . . .